Links in a chain

Links in a chain

An anthology of prose, poetry and plays

Compiled by

E M Murray

Academica

Copyright © 1991 E M Murray
Published by Academica,
a division of J L van Schaik (Pty) Ltd
1064 Arcadia Street, Hatfield, Pretoria
Illustrated by Antoinette Seymore
Cover design and chapter heads by Gibson Graphics
Typeset in 10 on 12 pt Century Schoolbook and
printed and bound by National Book Printers, Goodwood

ISBN 0 86874 427 1

No part of this book may be reproduced or transmitted in any form or by any means, electronic or mechanical, or by photocopying, recording or microfilming, or stored in any retrieval system, without the written permission of the publisher.

Contents

Introduction vii
1 Our dog 1
  Nothing – Eleanor Farjeon 1
  Dog – Diana Pitcher 2
2 Old things are useful too 6
  The kettle rhyme – Ian Serraillier 6
  Danny the champion of the world – Roald Dahl 8
3 Upside down 11
  Topsy-turvy world – William Brighty Rands 11
  The donkey, the miller and his son – Ian Ferguson 13
4 When winter comes 17
  Something told the wild geese – Rachel Field 17
  The timid starling – Paul Biegel (translated by Patricia Crampton) 19
5 Are you always obedient? 22
  Two people – E V Rieu 22
  Nombulelo – Marguerite Poland 24
6 Pride comes before a fall 29
  Lovely mosquito – Doug Macleod 29
  The scorpion – Hilaire Belloc 30
  The gingerbread boy – Helen Cresswell 31
7 Mischief 36
  I'd like to be a teabag – Peter Dixon 36
  The adventures of Pinocchio – Carlo Collodi (translated by Frances Wainwright) 38
8 Mrs Button and Mrs Frisby 43
  Mrs Button – James Reeves 43
  Mrs Frisby and the rats of NIMH – Robert C O'Brien 45
9 Quarrels 50
  The quarrel – Eleanor Farjeon 50
  The quarrel – Geraldine Elliot 51

10 The flood 56
    Old Noah's ark – American folk rhyme 56
    Boats sail on the rivers – Christina Rossetti 58
    The flood – Ruth Ainsworth 60
11 Are you brave? 65
    The icefall – Ian Serraillier 65
    Little John the Fearless – Italo Calvino (translated by Sylvia Mulcahy) 67
12 Going home 71
    Adventure – Harry Behn 71
    The new fire – Jenny Seed 73
13 Christmas 79
    Kings came riding – Charles Williams 79
    Long, long ago – Anonymous 81
    The goldsmith's daughter – Ian Ferguson 82
    Glossary 87
    Index of poets and writers 94

Introduction

To the Teacher

A knowledge of the structure of this anthology will enable the teacher to plan lessons effectively.
- Passages from three genres, namely poetry, prose and drama, are included. There are contributions from both South African and overseas writers who are considered to be leaders in the field of children's literature.
- The thirteen units focus on a variety of themes. Although the units need not be read in the order of presentation, a glance at the table of contents will indicate the relevance of some of them to a particular term during the year.
- Each unit contains one or two poems and a story or drama. A period of two to three weeks could be spent on each unit.
- When a difficult word occurs in the text, its definition, which relates to the context, appears as a footnote. A list of these words occurs again in alphabetical order in a glossary at the end of the anthology.

The focal point of teaching literature to young people should be the reading and enjoyment of the text itself. The questions are of secondary importance and some may even be omitted or replaced by others. However, a judicious selection of questions enables the teacher to judge the pupils' understanding and appreciation of a particular text. Not all the questions have a single, correct answer. Some should enable the pupil to relate the ideas expressed in literature to his own experiences of life.

The poems in this anthology have been written for children. Although they may not have quite the wide range of meanings encountered in poetry written for more mature readers, they should certainly elicit a wide range of responses.

Several poems are suitable for choral verse. Children enjoy reciting poetry and experience a feeling of security from the rhythmic patterns and sounds in a poem. This is an ideal opportunity for group work.

The plays may be read aloud and when the pupils become familiar with the text, parts may be allocated to different pupils reading in groups. A dramatic reading develops the pupil's awareness of meaning as expressed in tone of voice, volume and tempo of speech. A presentation to other classes in the school could be challenging and enjoyable.

The sections preceding and following the prose passages contain pre-reading activities, suggestions for discussion and writing tasks. Where applicable, pupils should engage in pair work and group work. The length of the stories varies, with the longer passages that require continuous concentration appearing towards the end of the anthology. The degree of difficulty varies in accordance with the large chronological, intellectual and linguistic variety that may exist in one class. In some instances, the prose passage is an extract from a longer work. A plot summary provides the necessary background. When pupils show particular interest in such a passage, the teacher should try to obtain the complete edition and read it to them.

It may be neither possible nor desirable for a teacher to use all the material in this anthology during one year. However, since the criteria of literary merit and joy in reading have been observed in its compilation, a teacher may select passages knowing that they will provide both pleasure and a worthwhile learning experience for the pupils.

E M Murray
Compiler

Our dog

Nothing

He's gone –
   and there is nothing.
Kind tones
   are nothing,
Butcher's bones
   are nothing,
The next-door cat
   is nothing,
Even his empty glove and hat
   are nothing,
The fighters in the street
   are nothing,
Friends, foes, and meat,
   all nothing, nothing, nothing –
He's gone,
   and I am nothing.

Eleanor Farjeon

tones – sounds of a voice
foes – enemies

Questions on the poem

1. Who is speaking? In line 1 when the speaker says, "He's gone", to whom is he referring?
2. Look at the title of the poem and notice how often it is repeated in the poem. What does it tell one about how the dog feels at this moment? When you read the poem aloud, what tone of voice will you use?
3. What is a dog's favourite food and what does he sometimes do with it?
4. Explain what a dog does when he sees a cat.
5. Who are the "fighters in the street"?
6. When will the dog feel happy again?
7. Write five or six sentences about your pet or a pet you would like to have. You should name the pet, describe what it looks like and explain how you look after it. Is your pet ever naughty? Does he make you laugh? Write a sentence telling about his naughty or funny ways.

PRE-READING ACTIVITY

Many people have dogs as pets. Try to find out for how many years dogs have been domestic animals. Discuss the ways in which dogs help man. Think about what a dog expects from his owner in return. If you have a dog you will know what makes it very happy. The poem 'Nothing' should help you.

Dog

Diana Pitcher

The winter was the coldest First Man could remember. The clouds, which usually covered the sky only in summer, had settled on the mountains, hiding the peaks for many days, and when they lifted and let Sun shine through again there was a glittering white cape on the mountain tops. Wind, who usually blew warmly from the plain to the mountains, changed her direction and came bustling and flurrying from the mountains to the plain. She was cold, colder even than the water had been at the bottom of the pool where First Man had lived when he was a serpent.

First Woman made cloaks of antelope skins for First Man and for Vugiswe and then one for herself, to try to keep out the cold, but even so they shivered whenever they left the hut.

It was so cold that even the animals of the plain began to wander further afield and soon there was little game to be seen anywhere. Only Hyena and Dog were left and they were both nearly starving. Hyena is used to following Lion and eating what Lion leaves, and Dog had always followed Hyena. Now Lion had gone and neither Hyena nor Dog could find any game small enough to attack for themselves. Each day they grew colder and hungrier until at last Hyena said, "Let us leave the plain as Lion has done. Let us follow Lion for I am dying of hunger." Together they set out.

Suddenly Dog stopped. He could smell meat, cooking meat, and the saliva dribbled from his mouth and his stomach rumbled. He knew where the smell came from. It came from First Woman's cooking pot. He also knew First Woman had no love for Hyena who often attacked the young calves of the herd or stole the fat young pullets as they scratched for food in the dusty earth. Dog knew that First Woman hated them; but he also knew that unless he ate soon he would die.

"Let us go to First Woman's hut, Hyena," he said. "Surely she will give us food."

"Are you mad?" answered Hyena. "Do you not know First Woman has Fire? Fire burns. It burns the ground around you, it burns the grass and the trees, it burns your paws, it singes the hair off your skin. I would rather die than approach Fire." And Hyena jogged on.

Dog raised his nose and smelled the meat again. He would risk Fire. Settling low on his belly, his front legs bent, his haunches only a little higher than his shoulders, he squirmed his way towards the smell of meat.

Now he could see First Man and First Woman and Vugiswe sitting round the orange flames which licked at the wood and ate it up, which cast eerie, flickering shadows across the grass towards Dog himself. It was true Fire would burn if it caught him, but if he could get just a little closer, not too close, but just a little closer, he would feel its warmth and there was just a chance that First Man or First Woman might toss aside a bone when they had eaten the meat off it.

Dog dropped even lower onto the ground and wriggled a little closer. He stopped and gave a tiny growl. First Man looked up. He saw the cringing creature but took no notice. No wild creature would approach too near to Fire.

Dog took one, slow step forward. He could just feel the warmth of Fire now. If he could get a little nearer perhaps the cold, frozen stiffness would leave his body. Even if he couldn't eat he could at least be warm. Vugiswe looked up. He rather liked the look of Dog, liked his smooth brown coat, his pointed black nose; but everyone knew Dog was wild and hunted with Hyena. Vugiswe bent forward and took another piece of meat from the cooking pot.

Very, very slowly dog took one step nearer; his tail gave one little wag. He whined. First Woman looked up. She saw Dog's thin, bony body and knew the hunger that gnawed at his stomach; she saw the trembling of his limbs and understood the cold that ate into his being. She looked into Dog's pleading eyes. They were not the eyes of a hyena or a jackal. They were eyes that told of courage, of love, of devotion.

She picked up a bone and held it out. Dog crawled nearer. Would First Woman strike him with it? Would she throw it at him? She still held the bone in her hand. He opened his mouth. She sat quite still. He took the bone. She moved that he might lie nearer the flames. She put out her hand very gently and patted his head. And Dog became man's slave.

> *peak* – top of a mountain
> *glittering* – shining brightly
> *serpent* – snake
> *starving* – dying of hunger
> *saliva* – the liquid in the mouth
> *pullet* – a young fowl
> *belly* – stomach
> *haunches* – part of the body around the hips
> *squirmed* – twisted the body
> *eerie* – strange and frightening
> *cringing* – moving away in fear
> *pleading* – asking or begging for something
> *courage* – bravery
> *devotion* – deep love
> *strike* – hit

Questions on the story

1 What do First Woman and First Man wear?
2 How do Dog and Hyena usually find food?
3 How does Dog know there is food nearby?
4 Explain why First Woman hates Hyena.
5 Why does Hyena refuse to go near First Woman's hut?
6 Explain what a wild animal does when he sees fire. What do dogs and cats do?
7 What difference does First Woman see between the eyes of Hyena and those of Dog?
8 First Woman is kind to Dog. Describe what she does.
9 The letters in the words below have been scrambled or mixed up. Put them in the correct order using the definitions given in the first column. All the words are in the story.

stomach ELYLB	b_____
mountain tops KPESA	p_____
very hungry TANRVGSI	s_____
a young fowl UEPLLT	p_____
bravery OUCAREG	c_____

Old things are useful too

The kettle rhyme

"My kettle's no use any more," mother said,
   Misery you, misery me,
And she hurled the hole-y thing over the hedge.
   Misery diddle fa-la!

A robin who found it flew down from a tree:
   Merrily you, merrily me,
"This'll do nicely for missus and me."
   Merrily diddle fa-la!

When father came home he was angry with mother:
   Misery you, misery me,
"I haven't the money to buy us another."
   Misery diddle fa-la!

Now robin and family happily settled,
   Merrily you, merrily me,
Peep out – all five – from the hole in the kettle.
   Merrily diddle fa-la!

Ian Serraillier

misery – unhappiness
merrily – joyfully, happily
robin – a small red-breasted bird
hole-y – having a hole in it

Questions on the poem

1 The robin makes a lovely home in the old kettle. In the next story you will read about a father and son who make a kite from an old blue shirt. Tell the class about something your mother or father threw away that you were able to use. Perhaps when you were small you and your friends dressed up in their old clothes and pretended to be grown-ups.
2 Why does mother throw away the kettle?
3 Mother throws the kettle over the hedge instead of into the dustbin. Who is pleased about this?
4 Explain why father is angry?
5 How many baby robins are born?
6 The words in Column A name objects used at home. The words in Column B describe their uses. Match the words in Column A with those in Column B.

Column A	Column B
jug	to contain tea
saucepan	to boil water
frying pan	to contain milk
kettle	to cook vegetables
teapot	to fry meat, eggs

PRE-READING ACTIVITY

Think of your best friend and of the times when you have a lot of fun together. What do you do? Sometimes you have to help your mother or father with a task at home. Tell the class about what you like doing best.

Danny the champion of the world
Roald Dahl

Danny's mother died when he was a baby. His father is a mechanic. Danny and he live near a small village in a brightly painted caravan behind the filling station and workshop.

And so life went on. The world I lived in consisted only of the filling-station, the workshop, the caravan, the school, and of course the woods and fields and streams in the countryside around. But I was never bored. It was impossible to be bored in my father's company. He was too sparky a man for that. Plots and plans and new ideas came flying off him like sparks from a grindstone.
"There's a good wind today," he said one Saturday morning. "Just right for flying a kite. Let's make a kite, Danny."
So we made a kite. He showed me how to splice four thin sticks together in the shape of a star, with two more sticks across the middle to brace it. Then we cut up an old blue shirt of his and stretched the material across the frame-work of the kite. We added a long tail made of thread, with little leftover pieces of the shirt tied at intervals along it. We found a ball of string in the workshop and he showed me how to attach the string to the frame-work so that the kite would be properly balanced in flight.
Together we walked to the top of the hill behind the filling-station to release the kite. I found it hard to believe that this object, made only from a few sticks and a piece of old shirt, would actually fly. I held the string while my father held the kite, and the moment he let it go, it caught the wind and soared upward like a huge blue bird.

"Let out some more, Danny!" he cried. "Go on! As much as you like!"

Higher and higher soared the kite. Soon it was just a small blue dot dancing in the sky miles above my head, and it was thrilling to stand there holding on to something that was so far away and so very much alive. This faraway thing was tugging and struggling on the end of the line like a big fish.

"Let's walk it back to the caravan," my father said.

So we walked down the hill again with me holding the string and the kite pulling fiercely on the other end. When we came to the caravan we were careful not to get the string tangled in the apple tree and we brought it all the way round to the front steps.

"Tie it up to the steps," my father said.

"Will it stay up?" I asked.

"It will if the wind doesn't drop," he said.

The wind didn't drop. And I will tell you something amazing. That kite stayed up there all through the night, and at breakfast time next morning the small blue dot was still dancing and swooping in the sky. After breakfast I hauled it down and hung it carefully against a wall in the workshop for another day.

grindstone – stone shaped like a wheel, used to sharpen tools
splice – join
brace – support
attach – join
soared – flew high up in the air
let out some more – allow more string into the air
the wind dropped – the wind blew gently
amazing – surprising
swooping – rushing
hauled – pulled

Questions on the story

1 Why was Danny never bored?
2 What kind of weather is needed for a kite to fly?
3 When the kite is high in the sky what does it look like? What did it feel like in Danny's hands?

4 The words in Column B are movements made by some creatures. Match them to the words in Column A.

   Column A   **Column B**
   fish   soars
   snake   burrows
   horse   swims
   bird   slithers
   worm   gallops

5 You may not yet have made a kite or a go-kart or, if you are a girl, have sewn a dress. But there are many tasks in the home that you have learned to do. In five or six sentences describe how to make a cup of tea, how to cook breakfast, how to clean up the yard. Think of other activities, mime one of them and ask the class to name the activity.

3 Upside down

Topsy-turvy world

If the butterfly courted the bee,
And the owl the porcupine;
If churches were built in the sea,
And three times one were nine;
If the pony rode his master,
If the buttercups ate the cows,
If the cat had the dire disaster
To be worried, sir, by the mouse;
If Mama, sir, sold the baby
To a gipsy for half a crown;
If a gentleman, sir, were a lady –
The world would be upside down.
If any or all of these wonders
Should ever come about,
I should not consider them blunders,
For I should be Inside-Out!

William Brighty Rands

topsy-turvy – upside down
courted – loved
buttercups – small plants with yellow flowers
dire – dreadful, horrible
gipsy – member of a race that has no permanent home
half a crown – twenty five cents
blunders – mistakes

Questions on the poem

1 Pretend that you and your teacher or you and your mother or father exchange places for one week. In a small group discuss what might happen. You could make up a story and act it.
2 Name some of the upside down events in the poem. Can you think of any other amusing topsy-turvy examples? The play *The donkey, the miller and his son* will give you one idea.

PRE-READING ACTIVITY

Are you the sort of person who likes to give advice? Are there times when it is better to remain silent? Discuss occasions when you were given advice by two different people. Was the decision you took the right one? Think of times when it would be better to say "No" instead of "Yes".

The donkey, the miller and his son
A play by *Ian Ferguson*

Characters

JACK the miller
TOM, his son
TWO GIRLS
AN OLD MAN
A PEASANT WOMAN
A FARMER
A DONKEY

Once there was a donkey who lived contentedly by a stream, near an old mill. One fine day, the first of May in fact, Jack the miller decided the time had come to sell the donkey so he called his son...

MILLER: Wake up Tom, show a leg. We're off to town to sell our donkey and we must get there early so we get the best price. *(So they packed a hamper for lunch and set off driving the donkey before them. Soon they came to a field where two girls were waiting to meet their boyfriends.)*

13

1ST GIRL: Look at those stupid men! They've got a fine donkey and instead of riding on his back, they crawl at his heels. What stupidity.
2ND GIRL: Hey stupid, why don't you ride to town? I bet if they had a coach they would run on behind it.
1ST GIRL: Well, choke in the dust if that's what you want. You could be riding in comfort.
(The miller felt most annoyed but he said nothing. When they were out of sight of the scornful girls, he stopped.)
MILLER: Tom, climb up and ride in comfort.
TOM: Oh! Righto!
(So Tom climbed onto the donkey's back and off they went. By and by they met an old man chewing tobacco in the sun.)
OLD MAN: There! That just goes to show what I've always said. This young generation doesn't show any respect for their elders and betters. Look at that boy riding like a lord while his poor father eats the dust that the donkey kicks up.
Come on, young man! Show some respect for your father. He's older than you are and knows more than you do. Let him ride, you can walk.
Really! These youngsters!
(And off he went. The miller was most upset.)
MILLER: Get down quickly son. The old man is right. It will look better if I ride and you walk.
(So his son dismounted and his father climbed onto the donkey's back. And on they went. After they had travelled in this manner for a mile or so, they passed a peasant woman returning from the market.)
WOMAN: OoooOH! Have you ever, your poor little boy is out of breath trying to keep up with the donkey. Shame!
If that was *my* son he wouldn't tire himself out trotting behind me. Selfish old man!
Shame!
You call yourself a father, you're not worthy to have children. It's your kind that make the world the kind of place it is.
Shame! *(and off she went.)*
MILLER: Oh dear, wrong again! Climb up behind me sonny and we'll see who can criticise us then.
TOM: Righto.
(And off they went. Presently they approached the house of a

wealthy farmer who was sitting on the stoep drinking his coffee.)
FARMER: Hey mister! Is that your donkey? Poor thing!
MILLER: Of course it is, why do you ask?
FARMER: I can't believe it. You are a disgrace. Nobody but a nincompoop would overload a beast like that. Don't you see how hard the ground is?
MILLER: Well we have to get to market somehow you know.
FARMER: You and your big son could quite easily carry the donkey. It would be easy for you and better for the donkey's feet.
MILLER: You know son, he's right. He works with animals all day, he should know what's what.
TOM: I thought he just sat drinking coffee all day, dad.
MILLER: Well, when he isn't drinking coffee he's feeding animals.
(And so, with a great deal of difficulty they tied the donkey's legs together and tied the donkey upside down to a branch cut from a nearby tree.)
MILLER: Now . . .
(panted the miller out of breath but very earnest . . .)
MILLER: Take one end of the pole, I will take the other and when I say heave, you'd better heave.
TOM: Righto, dad!
MILLER: Not far to go now, the market place's just the other side of the bridge.
(And off they went. Meanwhile the farmer had finished his coffee and telephoned his neighbours.)
FARMER: Quick neighbour, just look what is coming over the bridge to the market.
(Because it was a party line, lots of people listened in.)
1ST: They don't know much about animals! etc.
(But when they reached the middle of the bridge, the donkey's weight proved too much for them and they overbalanced and fell in. And so the miller and his son crawled out wet and sorry and the donkey swam to the other bank and went in search of daisies.)
MILLER: What a fool I was! I should never have tried to please everybody. They've all had the satisfaction of a good laugh and I've nothing at all for all my trouble.
TOM: Next time we'll do it the way you want to, dad.
MILLER: Yes, we will.
(And with that the miller boxed his son's ears, and they returned sadder but wiser to the mill by the stream.)

> *show a leg* – get out of bed
> *hamper* – large basket with a lid, used to contain food
> *annoyed* – angry
> *scornful* – showing no respect
> *peasant* – someone who works on the land
> *approached* – came near to
> *nincompoop* – foolish person
> *earnest* – serious
> *heave* – lift
> *party line* – a telephone line that is shared by several people
> *daisies* – white flowers with a yellow centre

Questions on the play

1 Which of these words are true of the girls? More than one word will be correct:
   critical, helpful, nosey, rude, friendly, scornful
2 According to the old man how should young people behave towards older people?
3 Of all the people who criticise the miller, who makes the silliest suggestions? Why then does the miller take the advice?
4 What lesson could we learn from this play?

4 When winter comes

Something told the wild geese

    Something told the wild geese
      It was time to go.
    Though the fields lay golden
    Something whispered – "Snow."
    Leaves were green and stirring,
      Berries, lustre-glossed,
      But beneath warm feathers
    Something cautioned, – "Frost."

      All the sagging orchards
      Steamed with amber spice,
    But each wild breast stiffened
      At remembered ice.
    Something told the wild geese
      It was time to fly –
    Summer sun was on their wings,
      Winter in their cry.

Rachel Field

> *stirring* – moving
> *lustre-glossed* – shining with a bright colour
> *cautioned* – warned
> *sagging* – sinking, hanging downwards
> *amber spice* – ripe, yellow fruit

Questions on the poem

1 When the seasons change wild geese *migrate* to another country. Turn to the next story, 'The timid starling', where you will find the meaning of the word *migrate* in paragraph five. Can you name other birds that do this? Do you know why they have to leave? Think of the food they eat.
2 Why are the fields "golden"? What might be growing there?
3 Which lines tell us that there is a lot of sweet-smelling fruit hanging from the branches?
4 Although we do not travel to another country when winter comes, there are some changes in our lives. Think of the longer hours of darkness, the warmer clothes we wear and the different sports we play. Write a few sentences on either the season you like best or the season you like least. Explain why you have chosen that particular season.

PRE-READING ACTIVITY

1 The word *timid* means easily frightened or shy. The opposite is *bold*. Can you think of occasions when a wild creature who is usually timid will suddenly become bold? Think of what happens in the story entitled 'Dog'.
2 Do you know these words?
  (*a*) To go away *from* one's own country to live in another is to e_____.
  (*b*) To come *into* another country to live there is to i_____

The timid starling

Paul Biegel

Starlings are noisy creatures. When a dozen of them sit in a tree, they sound like at least a hundred. They whistle and scream and croak all at the same time, until suddenly they take flight and go and land on another tree, where they find still more friends. Or they all fly up out of the trees at the same time; then there are at least a hundred or a thousand of them and it looks as if a dark cloud were sweeping across the sky. A crazy cloud, a magic cloud, which changes into a giant or an old woman or a billowing sea.

But Klee never wanted to join in. Klee was a timid starling who always hid himself away. He sat in nooks and crannies and never dared to join his screaming friends or fly with them in the magic cloud.

"Klee's a cowardy custard," they said, and, once they had said it, Klee was not even allowed to join in any more.

He didn't think that was too bad at first, but later, in the autumn, he thought it was very bad indeed, for it was then that the other starlings told him: "You can't migrate with us, either."

Migrate. That means make the great journey which the birds make before winter to the hot countries. They fly over oceans and mountains and forests until they have caught up with the summer weather, for they fly south when it is winter here.

"You stay here in your cranny," the starlings told Klee, "on your own. You are always on your own, after all."

Klee was upset, but he said: "Then I shall fly south on my own as well."

"Ha ha!" cried the others. "You can't do that. You don't know the way on your own and you will get tired much too quickly. You hardly ever fly."

And one shouted: "I bet you don't even know how!"

But Klee did know how to fly. Next morning, when all the other starlings had moved off with a lot of noise, he came out, took a last good look round for safety's sake, stretched out his wings and climbed towards the blue sky.

He flew and he flew and he flew. Straight on, but now and then a little bit to the left and little bit to the right. He flew over cities and forests and rivers. The cities were noisy, the forests were autumn gold and the rivers were like wriggling snakes.

19

But the south lay far away. However hard he peered, Klee could not see the summer anywhere. "Oof," he said, landing on a tall fence, "oof".

When it was dark, Klee felt very much alone. "I'm lost," he thought. "I shall never find the way." And he was tired. "If only I had a cosy nook," he thought, "I would stay in it all winter. I don't care any more."

He was a sad starling. And he was hungry.

Then Klee saw a little light in the distance. It was a house, a fine house with a crust of bread on the garden path and crumbs just under the window. Klee gobbled them up at once. Perhaps there would be still more on the window-sill. He was so hungry that he became a bold starling and sat right in front of the open window. But there was no bread on the window-sill. Instead, there was something else. A cosy nook.

A safe, dark nook, just the right size for a starling. Klee did not stop to think. He hopped towards it, jumped in, crept into the deepest corner, yawned an enormous yawn and fell asleep.

Klee's friends were by then already well on their way to the south. But birds are not the only things which fly that way.

People do too, in aeroplanes. And at the controls of an aeroplane sits a pilot. He is a man in a blue coat, and he wears a cap, a cap with a peak and a high front. So high that there is quite a nook inside it. The pilot of the aeroplane which was due to fly south that night had left home late. He had put his jacket on quickly, snatched up his cap from the window-sill and driven quickly to the airfield. So quickly that he did not notice how heavy his cap had become, as if there were something inside it. He didn't even notice as he raced towards the aeroplane to be in time, and once he was in the air he was too busy with all the little lights and dials. The aeroplane flew south in one night, high above all the birds flying in the same direction.

Not until the aeroplane had landed again, and the pilot got out after all the other people, did he think of his cap. "Oof," he said, "it's hot here." He took off his cap.

"Hey!" someone cried, "hey, just take a look at that!"

There were shouts and calls and laughter and everyone pointed at the pilot. For on top of his head sat a bird. A starling. A sleeping starling.

Klee was woken by the noise and in an instant he was flying, high in the air, the blue air of summer in the south.

Of course, Klee never realized how he had got there, but his friends were even more surprised.

For when they came flying in, tired out, three days later, they saw Klee perched happily in the highest tree.

> *nook* – a small, almost-hidden corner
> *cranny* – a small hole or crack
> *cowardy custard* – frightened, lacking courage
> *I bet* – I am sure
> *wriggling* – moving along by twisting to the left and right
> *peered* – looked very carefully
> *gobbled* – ate very quickly and greedily
> *perched* – rested

Questions on the story

1 Describe what the rivers looked like from the air.
2 At the house, what signs were there that the pilot cared for birds?
3 Why did the pilot not notice Klee?
4 Are these sentences true or false?
   (a) The noise made by a group of starlings is pleasant.
   (b) Klee wanted to migrate with the others.
   (c) A pilot wears a tight-fitting cap.

Are you always obedient? 5

Two people

Two people live in Rosamund,
    And one is very nice;
The other is devoted
    To every kind of vice –

To walking where the puddles are,
    And eating far too quick,
And saying words she shouldn't know,
And wanting spoons to lick.

Two people live in Rosamund,
    And one (I say it twice)
Is very nice *and* very good:
    The other's only nice.

E V Rieu

devoted – very interested in something
vice – wickedness, naughtiness
puddles – small pools of rainwater

Questions on the poem

1 Do you disobey your parents and teachers sometimes? What do you do? Tell the class about a time when you were disobedient and managed to escape punishment.
2 Rosamund is a disobedient child. Name some of her bad habits.
3 There are two lines in the poem telling us that the speaker likes Rosamund in spite of her naughtiness. Read those lines aloud.
4 The speaker in this poem is probably a grown-up who knows the naughty girl well. When you read the poem aloud which verse will you read in a rather cross, critical tone of voice? Why will you read it like this? Which verse should be read in a happy way?

PRE-READING ACTIVITY

1 Besides our parents and teachers there are others whom we should obey. Think of traffic rules and what the doctor or nurse tells us to do when we are ill. Discuss what might happen when a person is disobedient.
2 If you had to look after a younger brother or sister, what would you do if they disobeyed you?

Nombulelo

Marguerite Poland

Once, on a hillside, high above the river Kei, where the old brown boulders lie scattered and aloes bloom in winter, there lived two children called Mbulelo and Nombulelo.

One afternoon the mother of Mbulelo and Nombulelo called them to her and said, "Go, my children, and collect firewood so that I can cook our mealie-meal and beans. Take the path that leads across the hill and follow it until it forks at a place where an mphanga plant is growing. Listen carefully now," she said. "You must take the track to the *right,* for it will lead you to some wattle trees where you will find enough wood to carry home."

The children nodded and started off.

They walked along the edge of their mother's mealie-fields where the small grey doves search for fallen grain. Then they ran laughing and chasing each other into the open veld.

On and on they went until they saw the old mphanga plant which stood at the fork in the path. The track to the right looped down to a stand of wattle trees and the one to the left wound up to the crest of the hill where the red-grass bent against the sky.

Nombulelo stopped and looked about. "Which path is it that we should take?"

"The one to the right," said Mbulelo.

"No, no!" cried Nombulelo. "We must take *that* path – the one which climbs towards the sky. We should go to the left."

"Our mother told us to gather sticks near the wattle trees," objected Mbulelo.

"*You* may go that way," said Nombulelo, "but I shall not!"

And so they parted.

Up and up she climbed until she reached the crest of the hill. Then down the furthest slope she raced, where the aloes grow red among the rocks.

The sun was setting and the rocks hunched dark around her. Nombulelo was afraid. She hurried on, looking for a place where the wind had bent the red-grass against the sky; looking for the path where Ramba the puffadder had lain in the sand; looking for the mphanga plant which would show her the way home. But she could find none of them.

A small flame flickered in the undergrowth and its smoke was sweet with the smell of roasting mealies. Nombulelo crept towards it. At a three-legged pot, stirring it with a large wooden ladle, sat an old, old woman. She wore a long beaded fringe and the rough fur cap of a diviner and she chanted as she bent to her cooking.

Without looking up the old crone said to Nombulelo, "Ah, small one, I have heard you coming a long time – for do not lost calves bleat and stumble when they are searching for their kraal?"

"Yes," agreed Nombulelo fearfully.

"Come," the diviner beckoned her. "Taste."

Nombulelo knelt, eyes cast down and the old one, peering between the beads of her fringe, sat and watched as Nombulelo ate. Then she leaned across and pinched Nombulelo's cheek between two bony fingers. "Disobedient calves who wander have a wooden prong tied to their necks to keep them in the fields. Children who disobey their mothers are given tasks they must complete before they are rewarded!"

"Yes, Grandmother," whimpered Nombulelo.

"See," the old woman thrust a grindstone and a small basket of mealies at her. "You must grind these very fine. When you have finished, I will show you the way home."

"Yes, Grandmother," said Nombulelo meekly, eyeing the basket. It was not large. It was not even full. It would take no time at all to grind the mealies fine. Nombulelo took the grindstone, stripped the cobs and set to work.

"Sila, sila, sila! Grind, grind, grind," she sang. "Sila, sila, sila! Grind, grind, grind!" she chanted working slower, for her arms were small and not as strong as she had thought.

"Sila, sila, sila!" puffed Nombulelo, so intent on her task she did not notice the old woman replacing each mealie she had ground with another, taken from the folds of her cloak.

Nombulelo looked into the basket. The number of cobs remained the same no matter how fast she worked. She began to cry.

"Grind!" The old woman prodded her with her pipe. "Grind, or I shall not show you the way home!"

And so Nombulelo returned to her task and the old one sat in the firelight.

Not long after he left Nombulelo at the fork in the path where the mphanga plant grew, Mbulelo her brother entered the grove of trees where their mother had told them to gather wood. He collected a bundle, tied it together with a strip of bark and returned homewards. He hesitated when he reached the mphanga plant, wondering if he should climb the hill and search for his sister.

"She must have gone home," said Mbulelo to himself. But when he arrived at the homestead, it was deserted and only his mother's fowls pecked about the yard and his father's lean brown dog lay in the shade of the wall. He went a little way down the hill and there, below him, at a pool beneath the waterfall where the small waters of the Mvemve stream meet the great waters of the Kei, Mbulelo saw his mother with a bundle of washing.

"Mama, Mama," he cried. "Is Nombulelo with you?"

"No, my child," she said. "She is not here."

"She took the path," said Mbulelo, "that forks to the left of the mphanga plant."

"Hayi-bo!" cried his mother. "That is disobedience indeed!"

"And see," said Mbulelo, "the sun is setting and she will be alone in the dark."

"Come," said Mbulelo's mother, placing her washing in a basket and lifting it onto her head. "We must try and find your sister."

So they set out along the path that leads to the mphanga plant. The dog went ahead, nose to the ground, searching for the footprints of the child.

Down in the ravine the small Nombulelo was still grinding mealies.

"Sila, sila, sila," chanted the old crone, nudging Nombulelo. "Grind, grind, grind!"

Slower and slower went Nombulelo, the heels of her hands smarting from the rub of the grindstone. Slower and slower and slower until, unable to continue, she crouched down beside the fire and fell asleep.

The old woman smiled to herself and knocked out the ashes of her pipe against a log – a small sound like a woodpecker tapping on a tree.

The morning star is the last to leave the sky. It is called the milking star for it stays to light the way for those who milk the cows. It is as bright and warm as the first cooking-fire of the day. But no fire warmed the hearth in Nombulelo's home and no one went to tend the cows waiting in the kraal. For Nombulelo's mother and her brother Mbulelo still searched for her among the hills, calling as they pushed their way through thickets:

"Nombulelo. Nombulelo."

When Nombulelo woke she gazed around her in alarm. Where was the basket of mealies and the grindstone? Where was the old woman who had chanted as she bent to stir the cooking-pot? They had gone, and only a black-eyed lizard watched her from a stone.

Nombulelo scrambled up a hillside and paused, panting, where the first light of morning met the shadows of the valley. There were voices on the wind. Frightened, Nombulelo stopped to listen. From the dark ravine came the sound of faintest laughter. She climbed on hurriedly, glancing back every now and then in fear. Then suddenly, above her, a dark shape appeared on the brow of the hill. Nombulelo crept behind a rock, hid her face in her hands and wept.

As she wept, she heard familiar voices calling, calling: "Nombulelo, Nombulelo."

She peered timidly over the rock. Above her, dark against the morning sky, stood her mother and her brother Mbulelo. Mbulelo bounded down the slope towards her, while her mother waited for them on the ridge. Nombulelo ran to her, her arms outstretched as Mbulelo and her hunting-dog capered round them.

Wearily they turned for home, taking the path that forks beside the old mphanga plant. Nor did Nombulelo turn to gaze back up the hill where the wind bends the grass across the sky – for it somehow seemed to chant, "Sila, sila, sila, Nombulelo!" And the sound of quiet laughter was never far behind.

boulders – large rocks
crest – top
chanted – sang
crone – old woman
prong – long pointed stick
prodded – pushed or poked
homestead – house or hut with the land around it
ravine – deep valley
smarting – feeling painful
thickets – trees and bushes growing very close together
alarm – fear, fright
brow – top
familiar – well known

Questions on the story

1 Describe Nombulelo's duties at home.
2 To which animal does the old woman compare the disobedient Nombulelo?
3 Why does the old Grandmother make Nombulelo grind mealies?
4 For how long does Nombulelo sleep beside the fire and why is she frightened when she wakes up?
5 Which word best describes Mbulelo?
   (*a*) kind (*b*) reliable (*c*) friendly
6 Correct the words in brackets in the following sentences:
   (*a*) Nombulelo is (naughty) than her brother.
   (*b*) She climbed higher and higher until she reached the (high) spot on the mountain.
   (*c*) Nombulelo had to grind the mealies fine but the old woman ground them (fine).

Pride comes before a fall 6

Lovely mosquito

Lovely mosquito, attacking my arm
As quiet and still as a statue,
Stay right where you are! I'll do you no harm –
I simply desire to pat you.

Just puncture my veins and swallow your fill
For nobody's going to swot you.
Now, lovely mosquito, stay perfectly still –
A SWIPE! and a SPLAT! and I GOT YOU!

Doug Macleod

statue – stone figure of a person or animal
I'll do you no harm – I won't hurt you
desire – wish
puncture – prick a hole in something
veins – tubes that carry blood to the heart
swot – crush, squash, destroy

Questions on the poem

1 During which season of the year are we likely to be bitten by mosquitoes? Describe the mosquito's food and how you feel after being bitten.
2 Is the poet being truthful in the last two lines of the first verse? Which animals do we pat?
3 What happens to the mosquito? What does the word "SPLAT" tell us? Think of what the mosquito looks like at the end of the poem.

The scorpion

The scorpion is as black as soot,
   He dearly loves to bite;
He is a most unpleasant brute
   To find in bed, at night.

Hilaire Belloc

soot – very small black pieces found in the smoke of fires
brute – cruel beast

Questions on the poem

1 Have you ever found a scorpion in your bed or your shoe? If so, tell the class what you did.
2 We sometimes find other unwelcome creatures in our houses, for example, a mouse, a fly or a poisonous snake. Describe how you would get rid of each of these creatures.

PRE-READING ACTIVITY

1 You may have heard your parents use the proverb, "Pride comes before a fall". It means that when we think too much of ourselves we shall soon be in great trouble. If this has happened to you or to someone you know, tell the class about it.
2 Match the animal sounds in Column B with the animals that make these sounds in Column A.

Column A	Column B
cow	croaks
horse	quacks
dog	mews
cat	bleats
frog	barks
sheep	lows
duck	neighs

3 Choose the correct meaning of the word "lumber" in the following sentence:
As the hunter had only wounded the rhinoceros, he saw it *lumber* through the veld in great pain, crashing against low bushes.
(*a*) to walk swiftly
(*b*) to move in a noisy, clumsy way
(*c*) to fall to the ground.
The word "lumber" has another meaning. Consult a dictionary if you cannot remember it.

The gingerbread boy
Retold by *Helen Cresswell*

Once upon a time there was a little old woman who was making gingerbread. This old woman had never had any children of her own and had always longed for a little boy. So she said to her husband,

"I will make a little boy out of gingerbread. I'll knead the dough, and roll it, and cut out just the shape I want. Then I'll give him currants for his eyes and a slice of orange peel for a mouth, and I'll pop him in the oven and when he's nicely baked I'll take him out and I'll have a little boy of my own at last!"

The husband shook his head at his wife's words, and went off to work in the fields outside. The old woman did exactly what she had said she would do. She kneaded and rolled and shaped, and when at last the gingerbread boy was cooked she opened the oven door to take him out.

Before she could even blink out popped the little gingerbread boy of his own accord. He jumped out of the oven, ran out through the kitchen door and when he was in the street looked back over his shoulder and shouted,

"Run, run as fast as you can,
You can't catch me, I'm the gingerbread man!"

"Husband, husband, come quick!" cried the little old woman. And her husband came running from the field and they both ran after the gingerbread boy but they couldn't catch him.

As for the little gingerbread boy, he went running on and on till he met a cow eating daisies in a meadow. When the cow saw the little gingerbread boy, she said,

"Moo! Moo! You look good to eat! Stop, stop, little gingerbread boy, and let me eat you up!"

But the gingerbread boy only laughed and ran faster than ever, and as he ran he shouted over his shoulder,

"I have run away from a little old man and a little old woman, and I can run away from you, I can!

"Run, run as fast as you can,
You can't catch me, I'm the gingerbread man!"

The cow began to lumber after him, but she had eaten too many buttercups, and she couldn't catch him, either. So on and on he ran till he came to a horse drinking from a trough by the wayside. When the horse saw the little gingerbread boy he said,

"Neigh! Neigh! You look good to eat! Stop, stop, little gingerbread boy, and let me eat you up!"

But the gingerbread boy only laughed and ran faster than ever, and as he ran he shouted over his shoulder,

"I have run away from a little old man and a little old woman and a big fat cow, and I can run away from you, I can!

"Run, run as fast as you can,
You can't catch me, I'm the gingerbread man!"

And the horse began to gallop after him, but he couldn't catch him, either. The little gingerbread boy ran on and on till he came to some haymakers working in a field. They all began to shout to him,
"Hey, hey! You look good to eat! Stop, stop, little gingerbread boy, and let us eat you up!"

But the little gingerbread boy only laughed and ran faster than ever, and as he ran he shouted over his shoulder,
"I have run away from a little old man and a little old woman, and a big fat cow and a horse, and I can run away from you, I can!
"Run, run as fast as you can,
You can't catch me, I'm the gingerbread man!"

And the haymakers threw down their pitchforks, and began to run after him, but they couldn't catch him, either.

The little gingerbread boy ran on and on till he came to a river, and then he *had* to stop, because he didn't know how to swim. As he sat there wondering what he should do, along came a fox. The fox thought the little gingerbread boy looked good enough to eat, too, but he was clever enough not to say so. Instead, he grinned and showed his big yellow teeth, and said,

"Do you want to go across the river?"

"Yes, I do," said the little gingerbread boy.

"Jump on my back, then," invited the fox. "I can swim, and I'll take you across."

So the little gingerbread boy climbed on the fox's back and the fox began to swim across the river. When he was halfway over, the fox called out,

"You might get wet on my back, little gingerbread boy. Jump up on to my neck."

So the little gingerbread boy climbed on the fox's neck and the fox swam a bit further. Then he called out again,

"It can't be very comfortable clinging to my neck, little gingerbread boy. Jump on my head."

So the little gingerbread boy jumped on the fox's head and clung on tightly and the fox swam a bit further. Then he called out again,

"We're nearly there, now! Climb on to the tip of my nose for the rest of the way, you'll be safer there!"

So the little gingerbread boy climbed on to the tip of the fox's nose. And then the fox threw back his head and went "Snap" with his snapping jaws, and the little gingerbread boy was half gone. Then the fox did it again – "Snap" – the little gingerbread boy was three quarters gone. Then the fox did it once more – "Snap!" (oh, he was enjoying himself!) – and after that the little gingerbread boy was all gone. And that was the end of the gingerbread biscuit boy who had outwitted a little old man and a little old woman and a cow and a horse and a field full of haymakers, but hadn't been quite clever enough to outwit a fox!

> *knead* – to make flour and water into dough
> *of his own accord* – without being asked or helped
> *lumber* – to move clumsily and noisily
> *trough* – a box from which animals drink or feed
> *pitchfork* – a long-handled fork used to lift hay
> *outwit* – to get the better of someone by being cunning or clever

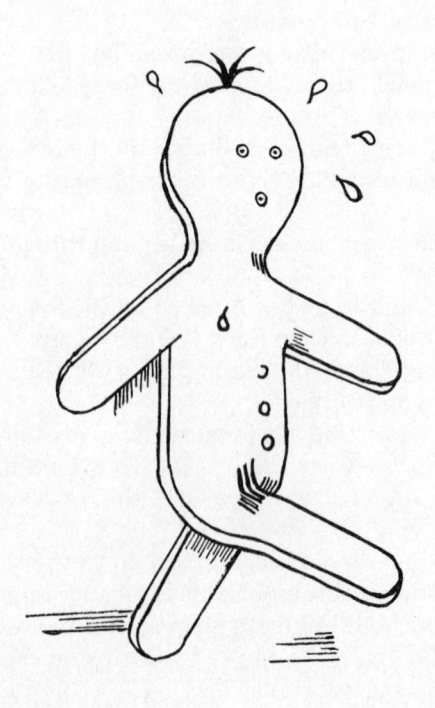

Questions on the story

1. Which word describes the character of the fox?
   (a) friendly   (b) helpful   (c) kind   (d) sly
2. The gingerbread boy says, "You can't catch me, I'm the gingerbread man." The words *can't* and *I'm* are shortened forms for *cannot* and *I am*. Another name for this is **contraction.** What are the contractions for the following?
   (a) I shall
   (b) she did not
   (c) he will
   (d) they could not
   (e) she is
   (f) we will not
   Write sentences using these contractions.
3. This is a lovely story to act. Form groups with eight or nine pupils in each group. These are the characters you will have: old man, old woman, gingerbread boy, cow, horse, two or three haymakers and the fox. You could take turns to act the part of the gingerbread boy.

Mischief 7

I'd like to be a teabag

I'd like to be a teabag,
And stay at home all day –
And talk to other teabags
In a teabag sort of way . . .

I'd love to be a teabag,
And lie in a little box –
And never have to wash my face
Or change my dirty socks . . .

I'd like to be a teabag,
An Earl Grey one perhaps,
And doze all day and lie around
With Earl Grey kind of chaps.

I wouldn't have to do a thing,
No homework, jobs or chores –
Comfy in my caddy
Of teabags and their snores.

I wouldn't have to do exams,
I needn't tidy rooms,
Or sweep the floor or feed the cat
Or wash up all the spoons.

I wouldn't have to do a thing,
A life of bliss – you see . . .
Except that once in all my life

I'd make a cup of tea!

Peter Dixon

Earl Grey – a type of tea
doze – sleep
chores – household jobs
comfy – comfortable
caddy – a small box containing tea
bliss – enjoyment, happiness

Questions on the poem

1 How does one know that the speaker in the poem was still at school?
2 Name the chores he had to do.
3 If he became a teabag, what would happen to him after he had made a cup of tea?
4 If you could become someone or something else for a day, what choice would you make? Tell the class about it. You should mention this person's name, the type of work he does and why you would like to change places with him.

PRE-READING ACTIVITY

Do you think that there is a difference between being naughty and hurting someone on purpose? Perhaps you can think of examples of both kinds of actions. Discuss whether things can be put right afterwards.

The adventures of Pinocchio
Carlo Collodi

Master Cherry the carpenter gave a piece of wood to his friend Geppetto who then made a wooden puppet so that the two of them could travel the world together and earn money.

Geppetto lived in a little room on the ground floor. It was lit by a small window under the stairs. His furniture could not have been simpler. One rickety chair, a shaky bed, and a broken-down old table. At the back of the room a fireplace could be seen with a good fire in it; but the fire was only painted, and over the painted fire was a painted pot, which was boiling merrily and sending forth clouds of steam, just like real steam.

As soon as he was home, Geppetto took up his tools and began to carve his puppet.

"What shall I call him?" he said to himself. "I think I'll call him Pinocchio because that name will bring him good luck. I once knew a whole family of Pinocchios and they all got along splendidly. The richest one of them was a beggar."

When he had thought of a name for the puppet he set to work with a will. He quickly made his hair, and his forehead, and his eyes.

As soon as the eyes were finished, he was amazed to see them move, and stare at him intently.

When Geppetto saw those two wooden eyes watching him, he didn't like it at all, and he said crossly: "Naughty wooden eyes, why are you looking at me?" But no one answered.

Next he made the nose; but as soon as it was finished it began to grow. It grew and it grew until it seemed as if it would never stop.

Poor Geppetto worked as fast as he could to shorten it, but the more he shortened it, the longer the nose became.

After the nose he made the mouth; but before he had finished it, it began to laugh and poke fun at him. "Stop laughing!" said Geppetto irritably, but he might as well have spoken to the wind.

"Stop laughing!" he threatened.

The mouth stopped laughing and then stuck out its tongue. Geppetto did not want to spoil the puppet, so he pretended not to see it, and went on with his work.

After the mouth he made the chin, then the neck, the shoulders, the stomach, the arms, and the hands.

The moment the hands were finished, Geppetto's wig was snatched from his head. He looked up. There was his yellow wig in the puppet's hands.

"Pinocchio! Give me back my wig this minute!"

But Pinocchio, instead of returning the wig, put it on his own head, and was almost hidden under it.

This insolence made Geppetto sadder than he had ever felt in his whole life. He turned to Pinocchio and said: "You rascal! I haven't even finished you yet, and already you're disobeying your father! That's bad, my boy, very bad indeed!"

And he wiped away a tear.

When Geppetto had finished the feet, a kick landed on his nose.

"It serves me right," he said to himself. "I should have thought of that before! Now it's too late."

He picked up the puppet and placed him on the floor to see if he could walk; but Pinocchio's legs were too stiff, and he didn't know how to move them. So Geppetto took him by the hand and showed him how to put one foot in front of the other.

When the stiffness wore off Pinocchio began to walk by himself, and run round the room; and finally he slipped out of the door and off he ran down the street.

Poor Geppetto ran after him as fast as he could but he could not catch him, for the little rascal leaped like a hare, and his wooden feet clattered on the pavement, making as much noise as twenty pairs of clogs.

"Catch him! Catch him!" cried Geppetto; but when the people in the street saw Pinocchio running by as fast as a racehorse, they stared at him in amazement, then they began to laugh and laugh until their sides ached.

At last, by some lucky chance, a policeman appeared. When he heard the noise he really thought a horse had got away from its master; so very bravely he planted himself in the middle of the street with his legs wide apart, determined to stop it and prevent any further trouble.

Pinocchio from far off saw the policeman and decided to run straight through his legs; but the policeman, without moving, picked him up neatly by the nose and returned him to Geppetto, who wanted to pull his ears to punish him. But to his annoyance he couldn't find any ears to pull. He'd been in such a hurry, he had forgotten to make him any.

So he grabbed him by the scruff of the neck, and as they walked away he said, threateningly: "Come home, I'll settle with you there!"

At this ominous remark Pinocchio threw himself on the ground and refused to budge. A crowd of busybodies soon gathered round him: "That poor puppet!" some of them exclaimed. "He is right not to want to go home! Who knows how dreadfully old Geppetto might beat him!"

And others added maliciously: "Geppetto *seems* a good man, but he is a perfect tyrant with children. If we leave that poor puppet in his hands, why, he's capable of tearing him to pieces!"

So the policeman let Pinocchio go free, and decided instead to put Geppetto in prison. Geppetto could say nothing in his own defence as he was crying like a calf that's lost its mother, and as they marched towards the prison he sobbed: "Wretched son! And to think I worked so hard to make him into a fine puppet! But I deserve it. I should have known what to expect!"

rickety – about to break
amazed – surprised
intently – seriously
irritably – crossly
wig – false hair sometimes worn when a person is bald
insolence – rudeness
rascal – mischievous person
clogs – shoes carved from wood
scruff of the neck – back of the neck
ominous – threatening
budge – move
maliciously – unkindly
tyrant – cruel ruler
sobbed – cried

Questions on the story

1 Complete the crossword puzzle. First write the answer next to the question. Then write it in *capital letters* in the crossword. All the answers can be found in the story.

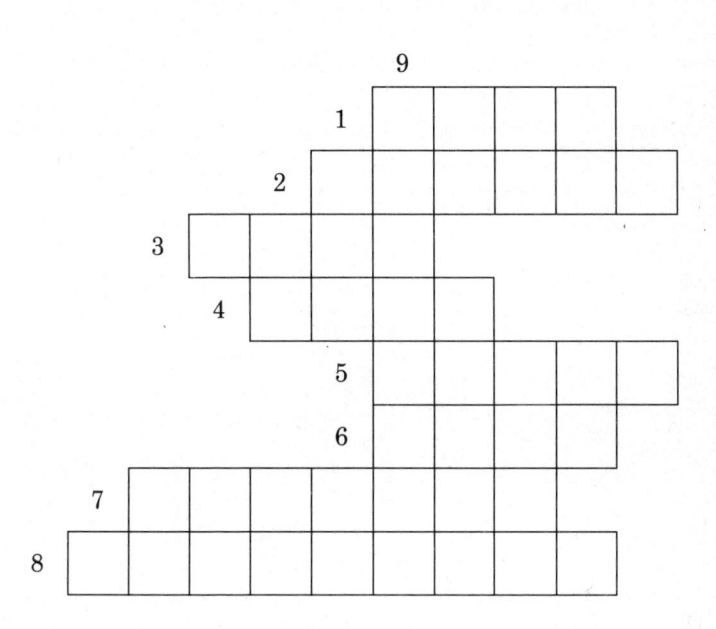

Across
(1) The plural of foot is f_____.
(2) It is very rude of Pinocchio to stick out his t_____ at Geppetto.
(3) This protects the head and should be combed. h_____
(4) Geppetto thinks these are naughty. e_____
(5) Pinocchio uses these to snatch Geppetto's wig from his head. h_____
(6) Geppetto forgets to make Pinocchio's e_____ .
(7) When Pinocchio is hungry he feels pain here. s_____
(8) Geppetto makes the s_____ after the neck.

41

Down
(9) This is the part of the face above the eyebrows. f_____

2. When Geppetto made Pinocchio's nose he found that the more he shortened it, the longer it became. Later on in the story he learned that the kinder he was, the naughtier Pinocchio became.
3. Can you complete these sentences in a similar way?
   (a) The more you eat, the _____ you will become.
   (b) The harder you work, the _____ your marks will be.
   (c) The earlier you start, the _____ you will finish.
   (d) The older you get, the _____ you walk.

8 Mrs Button and Mrs Frisby

Mrs Button

When Mrs Button, of a morning,
   Comes creaking down the street,
You hear her two old black boots whisper
   "Poor feet – poor feet – poor feet!"

When Mrs Button, every Monday,
   Sweeps the chapel neat,
All down the long, hushed aisles they whisper
   "Poor feet – poor feet – poor feet!"

Mrs Button after dinner
   (It is her Sunday treat)
Sits down and takes her two black boots off
   And rests her two poor feet.

James Reeves

> *chapel* – a small church
> *hushed* – silent
> *aisles* – passages between the rows of pews in a chapel or church

Questions on the poem

1 On which days are there services in your church? Why did Mrs Button sweep the chapel every Monday?
2 Explain why the aisles are silent. Where are most people on Monday mornings?
3 How do we know that Mrs Button worked hard throughout the week?
4 Read the poem again and decide which lines you will say very quietly. Which lines will you say in a whisper?
5 Match the words in Column A with those in Column B.

Column A	Column B
duster	sweep the floor
mop	clean the carpets
broom	wash the floor
tea towel	transfer dirt and dust to a dustbin
dustpan	dust the furniture
brush	dry the dishes

6 Write three or four sentences about the work your parents expect you to do at home. These are called chores. Explain when you do your chores and what you use to help you.

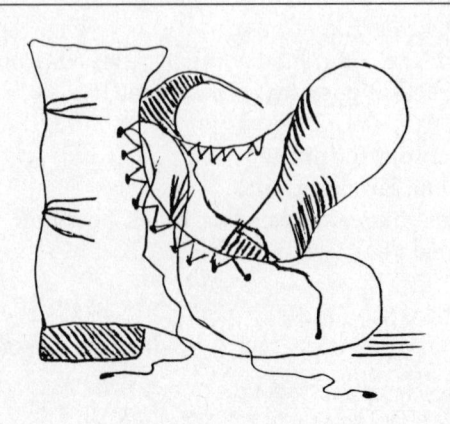

PRE-READING ACTIVITY

1 There is a proverb in English that you probably know. One good turn deserves another. Have you been in any difficulty lately? Who helped you overcome the problem? Think of ways in which you could repay this person for the kindness shown to you.
2 Column B is a list of animal homes. Match them to the words in Column A.

Column A	Column B
pig	kennel
cow	fold
horse	sty
dog	stable
fowl	byre
sheep	run

Mrs Frisby and the rats of NIMH
Robert C O'Brien

Mrs Frisby is a mouse living with her family of four children in Farmer Fitzgibbon's farmyard. When her son Timothy is ill, she obtains medicine from Mr Ages, an elderly mouse living on the other side of the farmyard. She now has to return home with the medicine before dark. But the cat is in the farmyard between her and safety.

The cat: He was called Dragon. Farmer Fitzgibbon's wife had given him the name as a joke when he was a small kitten pretending to be fierce. But when he grew up, the name turned out to be an apt one. He was enormous, with a huge, broad head and a large mouth full of curving fangs, needle sharp. He had seven claws on each foot and a thick, furry tail, which lashed angrily from side to side. In colour he was orange and white, with glaring yellow eyes; and when he leaped to kill, he gave a high, strangled scream that froze his victims where they stood.

Taking a firm grip on her packets of medicine, Mrs Frisby went under the fence and set out towards the farmyard. The first stretch was a long pasture; the barn itself, square and red and big, rose in the distance to her right; to her left, farther off were the chicken houses.

When at length she came abreast of the barn, she saw the wire fence that marked the other end of the pasture; and as she approached it, she was startled by a sudden outburst of noise. She thought at first it was a hen, strayed from the chicken yard – caught by a fox? She looked down the fence and saw that it was no hen at all, but a young crow, flapping in the grass, acting most oddly. As she watched, he fluttered to the top wire of the fence, where he perched nervously for a moment. Then he spread his wings, flapped hard, and took off – but after flying four feet he stopped with a snap and crashed to the ground again, shedding a flurry of black feathers and squawking loudly.

He was tied to the fence. A piece of something silvery – it looked like wire – was tangled around one of his legs; the other end of it was caught in the fence. Mrs Frisby walked closer, and then she could see it was not wire after all, but a length of silver-coloured string, probably left over from a Christmas package.

"Wait," said Mrs Frisby.

The crow looked down and saw her in the grass.

"Why should I wait? Can't you see I'm caught? I've got to get loose."

"But if you make so much noise again the cat is sure to hear. If he hasn't heard already."

"You'd make a noise, too, if you were tied to a fence with a piece of string, and with night coming on."

"I would not," said Mrs Frisby, "if I had any sense and knew there was a cat near by. Who tied you?" She was trying to calm the crow, who was obviously terrified.

He looked embarrassed and stared at his feet. "I picked up the string. It got tangled with my foot. I sat on the fence to try to get it off, and it caught on the fence."

"*Why* did you pick up the string?"

The crow, who was very young indeed – in fact, only a year old – said wearily. "Because it was shiny."

"You knew better."

"I had been told."

"Sit quietly," she said. "Look towards the house and see if you see the cat."

"I don't see him. But I can't see behind the bushes. Oh, if I could just fly higher . . ."

"Don't," said Mrs Frisby. She looked at the sun; it was setting behind the trees. She thought of Timothy and of the medicine she was carrying. Yet she knew she could not leave the foolish crow there to be killed – and killed he surely would be before sunrise – just for want of a few minutes' work. She might still make it by dusk if she hurried.

"Come down here," she said. "I'll get the string off."

"How?" said the crow dubiously.

"Don't argue. I have only a few minutes." She said this in a voice so authoritative that the crow fluttered down immediately.

"But if the cat comes . . ." he said.

"If the cat comes, he'll knock you off the fence with one jump and catch you with the next. Be still." She was already at work with her sharp teeth, gnawing at the string. It was twined and twisted and twined again around his right ankle, and she saw she would have to cut through it three times to get it off.

As she finished the second strand, the crow, who was staring towards the house, suddenly cried out:

"I see the cat!"

"*Quiet!*" whispered Mrs Frisby. "Does he see us?"

"I don't know. Yes. He's looking at me. I don't think he can see you."

"Stand perfectly still. Don't get in a panic." She did not look up but started on the third strand.

"He's moving this way."

"Fast or slow?"

"Medium. I think he's trying to figure out what I'm doing."

She cut through the last strand, gave a tug, and the string fell off.

"There, you're free. Fly off, and be quick."

"But what about you?"

"Maybe he hasn't seen me."

"But he will. He's coming closer."

Mrs Frisby looked around. There was not a bit of cover anywhere near, not a rock nor a hole nor a log; nothing at all closer than the chicken yard – and that was in the direction the cat was coming from, and a long way off.

"Look," said the crow. "Climb on my back. Quick. And hang on."

Mrs Frisby did what she was told, first grasping the precious packages of medicine tightly between her teeth.

"Are you on?"

"Yes."

She gripped the feathers on his back, felt the beat of his powerful black wings, felt a dizzying upward surge, and shut her eyes tight.

"Just in time," said the crow, and she heard the angry scream of the cat as he leaped at where they had just been. "It's lucky you're so light. I can scarcely tell you're there. Where do you live?".

"In the garden patch. Near the big stone."

"I'll drop you off there." He banked alarmingly, and for a moment Mrs Frisby thought he meant it literally. But a few seconds later – so fast does the crow fly – they were gliding to earth a yard from her front door.

"Thank you very much," said Mrs Frisby, hopping to the ground.

"It's I who should be thanking you," said the crow. "You saved my life."

"And you mine."

"Ah, but that's not quite even. Yours wouldn't have been risked if it had not been for me – and my piece of string." And since this was just what she had been thinking, Mrs Frisby did not argue.

"We all help one another against the cat," she said.

"True. Just the same, I am in debt to you. If the time ever comes when I can help you, I hope you will ask me. My name is Jeremy. Mention it to any crow you see in these woods and he will find me."

"Thank you," said Mrs Frisby. "I will remember."

Jeremy flew away to the woods, and she entered her house, taking the three doses of medicine with her.

> *apt* – suitable
> *fangs* – long, sharp teeth
> *shedding feathers* – letting feathers fall
> *embarrassed* – feeling uncomfortable
> *dubiously* – in doubt
> *authoritative* – having the power to make others obey
> *panic* – fear
> *banked* – turned with one wing higher than the other

Questions on the story

1 Which words tell us Dragon is dangerous?
2 Why is Jeremy the crow unable to fly away and what will happen to him if Mrs Frisby fails to gnaw through the string?
3 Why is it so important for Jeremy to make no noise?
4 Explain why the crow was so interested in the piece of string.
5 Describe how Jeremy saves Mrs Frisby's life.
6 From each of the following lists of words choose the one that does *not* belong.

(a)	(b)	(c)
gigantic	gnaw	panic
enormous	chew	sad
narrow	munch	fright
great	lick	terror
huge	bite	fear

7 If you had to describe Mrs Frisby's character, what would you say about her?

Quarrels 9

The quarrel

I quarrelled with my brother,
I don't know what about,
One thing led to another
And somehow we fell out.
The start of it was slight,
The end of it was strong,
He said he was right,
I knew he was wrong!

We hated one another.
The afternoon turned black.
Then suddenly my brother
Thumped me on the back,
And said, "Oh, *come* along!
We can't go on all night –
I was in the wrong."
So he was in the right.

Eleanor Farjeon

fell out – became bad friends
slight – unimportant
thumped – beat, hit

Questions on the poem

1 Have you had a quarrel with someone recently? Can you remember what you argued about?
2 There are two lines in verse 1 telling the reader that the quarrel is about an unimportant matter. Read these lines aloud.
3 Which line tells one that the brothers are unhappy?
4 To apologize means to say that you are sorry. Who apologizes first in this poem? Why does the poet say "he was in the right"?

PRE-READING ACTIVITY

1 Think of something that makes you feel angry. Perhaps it is a habit that your friend, brother or sister has. Is there something that you do or say that upsets others? Discuss how you settle your differences. Do you fight, talk, sulk or laugh about it?
2 Choose the correct answer.
 The phrase "bringing up the rear" means
 (*a*) to walk first   (*b*) to come last   (*c*) to walk in twos.

The quarrel
Geraldine Elliot

"Che! Che! Cheka, cheka, che!" sang the Honey-guide, as he flew in and out of the trees that grew beside the narrow track through the bush. "Che! Che! If you want honey, I can guide you to it!"

"Honey?" said a youth who was walking along. "I should like some honey. I will follow you. Lead on Nsadzu."

So the little grey bird darted on and the youth, whose name was Ndodo, followed him. And they had not gone very far when they saw Tambala, the Cock, who was scratching about in the path in search of food.

"Good morning," said Tambala. "Where are you off to in such a hurry?"

"To get some honey," answered Ndodo.

"Honey? In a honeycomb?"

Ndodo nodded.

"Then I'm coming with you," and Tambala gave a loud crow,

just to show how pleased he was, and ran along behind the youth and the Honey-guide.

The track wound on, twisting and turning through the trees and scrub. On either side grew yellow daisies and tall grass, with here and there a lovely purple iris or a wild larkspur. Suddenly a bush-cat dropped from a tree, stopped abruptly in the middle of the path and demanded to know where the Youth and the Cock and the Honey-guide were all going.

"To get some honey," said Ndodo promptly. "Do you want to come too?"

"*Do* I want to come!" exclaimed Bush-cat. "What a question! Why, honey is my favourite food." And she licked her lips and scuttled along beside Tambala, murmuring ecstatically to herself the one word: "Honey."

A little further on they saw a Duiker breakfasting off the tender leaves of the Dema shrub.

"Morning, Duiker," said Ndodo, as he passed.

"G'morning," replied Duiker with his mouth full. "Where are you going with Nsadzu, and Tambala, and Bush-cat, if I may ask?"

"We are going to get some honey."

"Oho!" said Duiker. "In that case I'm coming with you. Who wants leaves for breakfast when there's honey to be had?"

Chattering of this and that they hurried on, down a gully and across a stream, and there, at the water-hole, was Nyalugwe, the Leopard, drinking his fill. He lifted his head and looked at the little party.

"Hullo! Hullo!" he said, "What's all this about? Where are you off to in such a hurry? You, and Nsadzu, and Tambala, and Bush-cat, and Duiker?"

"To get some honey," came the answer.

"Indeed?" said Nyalugwe. "Then I think that I will come with you," and he climbed gracefully up the bank of the stream and stalked along beside Duiker.

Further on they were joined by Nchefu, the Eland, and Mkango, the Lion, and while Nododo was telling them about the honey, they heard an indignant snort close by and saw Njobvu, the Elephant, coming slowly towards them, waving his trunk to and fro.

"What's all this noise?" he demanded crossly. "Never heard anything like it. If you *must* talk, why can't you talk quietly? You woke me up just when I was having a most refreshing sleep."

"Sorry, Njobvu, but we didn't know you were there."

"Where are you going, you and Nsadzu, and Tambala, and Bush-cat, and Duiker, and Leopard, and Eland, and Lion?"

"We are going to get some honey. Would you like to come too?"

"Honey? Did you say 'honey'?" asked Njobvu, a low smile spreading all over his wrinkled face. "*Would* I like to come, too! Of course I am coming."

The Honey-guide flew on and the little procession followed with Njobvu, the Elephant, bringing up the rear. Suddenly Nsadzu settled on the branch of a tree.

"Che! Che! Cheka, cheka, che!" he sang again. "If you want honey, here it is!"

And there, sure enough, was the honey – four beautiful waxy combs of golden-brown honey.

Quickly Ndodo made four little platters from the bark of the tree, and when he had extracted the honeycombs, oh so carefully, he put one comb on each platter. The first he gave to the Cock and the Bush-cat; the second to Duiker and Leopard; the third, to Eland and Lion; and the fourth he kept for himself and Njobvu, the Elephant.

"Come now, let us eat," he said.

Then the Cock started to scratch at his end of the comb, and Bush-cat started to lick at hers; and Duiker ran his long tongue all round the second comb, while Leopard clawed at it; and Eland chewed and chewed at her end of the third comb, while Lion tore a great piece off with his teeth; and in less than no time they had all grown very angry and stopped eating. Bush-cat simply bristled all over with indignation.

"Really!" she said to the Cock. "What a disgusting way to eat – scratching with your talons like that! Have you no manners, Tambala? Don't you know how to eat properly?"

"I like that!" exclaimed Tambala, angrily fluffing up his feathers. "You're a nice one to talk! What do you think you are doing, licking the honeycomb all over and making it quite unfit for a decent bird to eat?"

"I flatter myself that my manners are as good as anybody's," said Bush-cat stiffly, "and . . ."

"You *do* flatter yourself, then," retorted Tambala.

"Oh! How dare you!" with a scream of rage, and extended claws, Bush-cat struck out at the Cock, who ducked and did his best to peck her in return.

Meanwhile, Nyalugwe, the Leopard, was objecting very strongly to the way in which Duiker ate, and Lion was objecting to the way in which Eland ate and very soon they, too, were quarrelling and fighting.

"My friends! My friends!" cried Ndodo. "You must not quarrel like this! Make up your differences, I beg of you, and let us eat our honey in peace."

"I won't eat with Tambala," cried Bush-cat at once.

"I won't eat with Duiker," snarled Nyalugwe, the Leopard.

"I won't eat with Eland," roared Mkango, the Lion.

"And I won't eat with you," said Njobvu, the Elephant, and he seized the honeycomb in his trunk, popped it into his mouth and ate the whole of it himself.

Then Ndodo was very angry indeed and he picked up his bow and arrow (which he'd put down beside the tree of the honeycombs) and, fitting an arrow to it, he took aim at the Elephant.

"Now," he said, in a voice of thunder, "this is the first time that there has been quarrelling amongst us. I do not like it and I intend to be obeyed. If you do not stop fighting at once, I will shoot."

At that the animals did stop, and in silence they looked at Ndodo and his bow and arrow. Then:

"Very well," said Njobvu, crossly. "We will stop fighting, but from now on we shall never cease to be enemies, Tambala and Bush-cat, Duiker and Leopard, Eland and Lion, and myself and

Man." And, as if he were uttering a challenge, he trumpeted loudly, turned, and disappeared into the bush, while the other animals all ran away in different directions.

Ndodo sighed. Then he looked sadly at the ruined honeycombs. "Che! Che! Cheka, cheka, che!" sang the Honey-guide above him. "If you want honey, I will lead you to it! But do not bring others with you. This time you and I will go alone!"

Still singing gaily, the little grey bird flew off. After a moment's pause Ndodo followed.

iris – plant with blue flowers
larkspur – tall plant with white, pink or blue flowers
promptly – at once
ecstatically – joyfully
indignant – angry
procession – a number of people following each other
the rear – back part
platter – large, flat dish
extracted – took out
flatter – praise very much
rage – anger
extended – stretched out
cease – stop
trumpet – noise made by an elephant

Questions on the story

1 Explain why the animals quarrel.
2 What noise does the elephant make?
3 What lesson is the writer trying to teach in this story?
4 If you form groups of nine pupils per group you can act out this story.
   These are the characters:
   Nsadzu, the Honey-Guide   Nyalugwe, the Leopard
   Ndodo, the Youth   Nchefu, the Eland
   Tambala, the Cock   Mkango, the Lion
   The Bush-cat   Njobvu, the Elephant
   Duiker

The flood

10

Old Noah's ark

Old Noah once he built an ark,
And patched it up with hickory bark.
He anchored it to a great big rock,
And then he began to load his stock.
The animals went in one by one,
The elephant chewing a caraway bun.
The animals went in two by two,
The crocodile and the kangaroo.
The animals went in three by three,
The tall giraffe and the tiny flea.
The animals went in four by four,
The hippopotamus stuck in the door.
The animals went in five by five,
The bees mistook the bear for a hive.
The animals went in six by six,
The monkey was up to his usual tricks.
The animals went in seven by seven,
Said the ant to the elephant, "Who're ye shov'n?"
The animals went in eight by eight,
Some were early and some were late.
The animals went in nine by nine,
They all formed fours and marched in a line.
The animals went in ten by ten,
If you want any more, you can read it again.

American folk rhyme

> *ark* – the ship built by Noah that saved him from the Flood
> *hickory* – a tree with very heavy wood
> *stock* – animals
> *caraway bun* – a bun with the seeds of the caraway plant
> *hive* – beehive, home for bees
> *"who're ye shov'n?"* – Who are you pushing?

Questions on the poem

1 Can you remember where the story of Noah's ark can be found? Genesis, the first book of the Bible, chapters 6 to 9, contains the story of the Flood. If your teacher reads chapter 7 to you, you will notice a difference between the words of the Bible and the poem.

2 Name the smallest animals mentioned in the poem. Do you think that the elephant is really trying to push the ant over? Why does the ant say this then?
3 Which animal is the largest? Why does the hippopotamus get stuck in the door?
4 There are manay interesting ways of reading this poem aloud. Small groups of readers could read two lines each. Or the whole class could read the lines beginning "The animals went in" and individual pupils could read the other lines.
5 If you have been to a zoo you will be able to think of other animals not mentioned in the poem. Describe one and ask the class to identify it.
6 Make a class picture of this poem. A small group of pupils should draw and colour in a very large ark. Each pupil can choose an animal to draw, cut out and stick onto the class picture. Remember to include the rainbow. The next poem, 'Boats sail on the rivers' is about a rainbow. If you cannot remember the colours of a rainbow read question 3 that follows the poem.

Boats sail on the rivers

Boats sail on the rivers,
   And ships sail on the seas;
But clouds that sail across the sky
   Are prettier far than these.

There are bridges on the rivers,
   As pretty as you please;
But the bow that bridges heaven,
   And overtops the trees,
And builds a road from earth to sky
   Is prettier far than these.

Christina Rossetti

bow – rainbow
overtops – to rise above something

Questions on the poem

1 When was the last time you saw a rainbow? Can you remember what the weather was like? Perhaps you can explain to the class why a rainbow appears in the sky.
2 The former poem is about Noah's ark and the Flood. Your teacher may have read some verses from the Bible. Read Genesis chapter 9, verses 12-17 and discover why the rainbow is so important.
3 Why does the poet say that a rainbow is prettier than a bridge on the river? Do you know the colours of the rainbow? They are red, orange, yellow, green, blue, indigo, violet.

PRE-READING ACTIVITY

1 On television and the radio you may have seen and heard of floods. Perhaps you live in an area that has been flooded. Discuss what you saw. What can people do when threatened by floods?

2 Match the expressions in Column A with their meanings in Column B.

Column A
to drag one foot after the other
to have hardly a wink of sleep
to do something as quick as a flash
to say that someone has nine lives

Column B
to act swiftly
to overcome all dangers
to walk in an exhausted way
to have very little rest

3 Name the young of these animals. The first letter has been given to you.

cat   k_____
dog   p_____
horse   f_____
cow   c_____
sheep   l_____
lion   c_____

The flood

Ruth Ainsworth

Minnie the mother cat and her three new-born kittens, One, Two and Three were in a box in the garden shed. One night a storm blew up and the river at the bottom of the garden overflowed its banks. The river continued to rise until the water reached the shed.

Suddenly there was a clap of thunder and a great blast of wind. The door of the shed blew open with a bang. The water rushed in and the box swirled round and round. Then it floated out of the shed into the garden.

The river had risen so high that it swept over the garden wall. The box swished over the wall and sailed along the river which was now wide and deep like a sea. It was too dark to see exactly where they were going. Minnie cuddled her babies close to her while the rain fell in torrents. The kittens were soon fast asleep, and though Minnie was sure she would never get a wink herself, she dozed off as well.

When morning came, they were in a watery world. There was water in front of them. Water behind. Water all round. Minnie did not know there could be so much water in one place. Strange things floated by. Branches of trees which had been torn off by the storm. Tables and chairs and pillows and cushions that had been washed out of houses. Sacks and straw and even a dog-kennel. Minnie was pleased to see that the kennel was empty.

Nothing stopped Minnie from bringing up her kittens as well as she could, so she washed them just as carefully as if they had been on dry land. When she had finished One's face, he mewed in an excited voice:

"I can see! I can see! I can see you and Two and Three and the water and everything!"

He frisked about with joy and Minnie was afraid he might fall out of the box.

Before long, Two and Three could see as well and they spent most of the day calling out:

"What's that? What's that? What's that?" or else: "Why is the water shiny? Why is it brown?" and many other questions, some of which Minnie could not answer.

Now that the rain had stopped the floods began to go down. The river was no longer wild and roaring. Hedges and bushes could be seen that had been under water a few hours before. When the box drifted near the bank and was caught on the branches of a willow tree, Minnie knew what she must do.

Quick as a flash, she snatched up the nearest kitten who happened to be Two, and climbed up the tree with him. She dashed back for One and Three and the little family were soon perched on the damp, slippery branch of a willow, instead of cuddled in a floating cradle filled with straw.

"This is a horrid place!" mewed One.

"I shall fall into the water and be drowned!" mewed Two.

"How are we to sleep without a bed?" mewed Three.

Minnie was not comfortable herself as she was trying to look after three young kittens as well as hold on, but she did not approve of grumbling.

"The river is going down," she said cheerfully. "Tomorrow or the next day I shall carry you home, one at a time, in my mouth. Till then, you must be good kittens and do what I tell you."

"Do you know the way home?" asked One. "We must have

floated a long way in our wooden box."

Minnie was not certain that she *did* know the way, but she replied firmly:

"Of course I know the way. The river brought us here. I shall just follow the river and it will lead us home. Anyhow, all sensible cats know the way home. They never get lost."

All day and all night Minnie took care of her kittens. She fed them and washed them and sang to them, and when they slept she kept them from falling off the branch. When they were awake and wanted to play, she told them stories. She told them about the red kitchen fire that ate black coal. She told them about mice with long tails who lived in holes and were fun to chase. She told them about dear Mrs Plum and her white apron and her warm, comfortable lap.

When the *next* morning came, the river had gone right down. The ground was wet and muddy, but it was not under water. They could see the path running along the river bank.

"I shall take one of you home now," said Minnie.

"Take me! 'No, me! No, ME!" mewed the three kittens.

"I shall take Three first because she is the smallest," said Minnie. "Now One and Two, be brave and sensible and hold on tightly."

"What will happen if we fall off?" asked One and Two.

"You would lose one of your nine lives," said Minnie. "Then you would have only eight left."

She took little Three in her mouth, climbed down the tree to the ground, and ran off along the river bank. She felt sure she was going the right way and that every step was bringing her nearer home. The wet mud was cold and nasty to her feet, but she did not mind. If only her three kittens were safe in front of the kitchen fire, she would never mind anything again!

Little Three seemed to get heavier and heavier. When at last Minnie padded slowly through the gate, and up the path to the back door, she could hardly drag one foot after the other.

"Miaow! Miaow!" she cried as loudly as she could. "Miaow!"

In a second the door opened and there stood dear Mrs Plum in her white apron.

"Oh, Minnie! Minnie!" she cried, gathering Minnie and Three up in her arms, and not minding at all about the mud they left on her apron. "I thought I should never see you again!"

At first Minnie purred loudly and smiled, but she knew the job was not yet finished. She began to kick and struggle till Mrs Plum put her down on the floor. Then she ran to the back door and mewed for it to be opened.

"I know," said Mrs Plum. "I understand. You must go back for the others. Wait a moment and I will come too, I'll just make Three safe and comfortable. I kept a bed ready for you all."

There, on the hearth-rug, was another box with a soft blanket inside. Mrs Plum cuddled Three into the blanket, and Three sat and stared at the fire with round blue eyes. So *this* was the monster who ate black coal!

Mrs Plum put on her coat and hat and took a basket with a lid and opened the door. Minnie ran ahead so quickly that Mrs Plum could only just keep up. They were both tired when they got to the willow tree. Mrs Plum stood at the bottom while Minnie climbed up and found her two kittens cold and shivering, but quite safe.

"We've kept all our nine lives, Mother!" they called out.

"That's my good kittens!" said Minnie, carrying them down to the ground, where Mrs Plum stroked them and petted them and tucked them into the basket, which was lined with flannel. There was just room for Minnie as well. Then Mrs Plum carried the heavy basket home. She had to change hands when one arm ached.

When they were back in the warm kitchen, Mrs Plum gave Minnie a good meal. She had sardines and a dish of corn-flakes and three saucers of milk. Then they all five settled down for a cosy afternoon by the fire. Mrs Plum knitted in her rocking chair, and the three kittens watched the red fire eating coal and stared at the brass rim of the fender and the plates on the dresser and all the other wonderful things.

They kept looking at Mrs Plum's ball of wool.

"I don't know why, but I should like to roll that ball of wool all over the floor," said One.

"So should I!" said Two and Three.

"That would be very naughty of you indeed," said Minnie. "But I wanted to do just the same when I was a kitten."

"And did you do it?" asked the three kittens.

"Yes, I'm afraid I did!" said Minnie.

She purred and smiled and dozed, as the clock ticked on the wall and the fire crackled and Mrs Plum clicked her knitting needles.

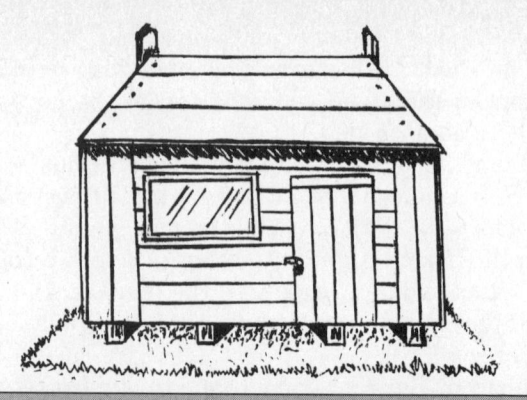

swirled – twisted
rain fell in torrents – heavy rain fell
frisked – ran about in a playful way
damp – wet
approve – agree with
flannel – soft woollen cloth
fender – piece of metal around a fireplace to prevent burning coal from falling onto the floor

Questions on the story

1 The box floats on the water. What is it made of?
2 The kittens ask Minnie why the floodwater is brown. Do you know why?
3 Describe how a cat carries her kittens.
4 Even though Minnie is not sure of the way home she tells the kittens that cats never get lost. Why does she say this?
5 Why does Three go home first?
6 Describe how One and Two return home.
7 Choose the word that does *not* describe Minnie.
   (a) sensible   (b) determined   (c) foolish
   (d) brave
8 Say whether these sentences are true or false.
   (a) Kittens are born blind.
   (b) Cats like water.
   (c) The cat is the enemy of the mouse.

11 Are you brave?

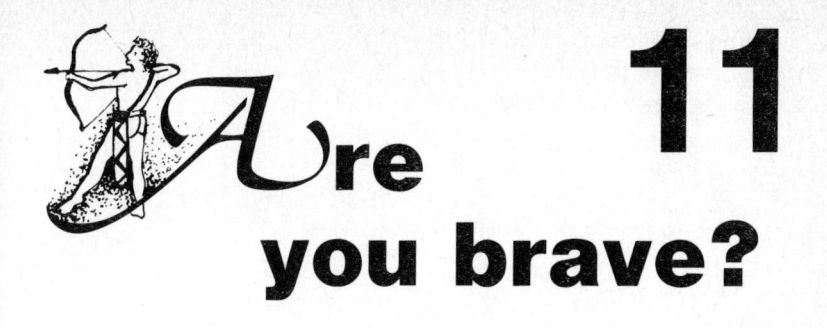

This poem, 'The icefall', describes how in May 1953, Edmund Hillary and Sherpa Tenzing were the first to climb Mount Everest, the highest mountain in the world.

The icefall

    Then Hillary attacked. Snow falling, wind howling,
    Five days he fought, with axe and hoisting gear,
    Ladder of aluminium, ladder of rope
    And timber for bridging. Time and again
5 They were beaten back –
    When cliff and wall crumbled, when avalanche
    Wiped out a hundred feet of track,
    By crevasse and gaping chasm, by toppling pinnacle
    And serac overhanging. But they fought back.
10 Hack, hack at the ice! Over that ridge now –
    Here's a flag to mark it – keep to the left of this –
    We'll fix a line to the wall there – watch for the abyss.
    Hack, hack at the ice! It was the same every day
    Till they pitched a couple of tents on a shelf half way.

15 Hack, hack at the ice! More ridges,
    Crevasses and pinnacles and chasms and bridges.
    Hack, hack at the ice! or wade in the snow knee-deep

And battle to the top. At 20,000 there was room,
Just room to pitch a tent and, over the brink above, peep
20 Into their dreams and longings, into the Western Cwm.

Ian Serraillier

hoisting – lifting
timber – wood
avalanche – a mass of snow, ice and earth that falls swiftly down a mountain
crevasse – deep opening in ice or rock
chasm – deep opening in ice or rock
pinnacle – peak, high part of a mountain
serac – hill of ice
abyss – a very deep hollow
cwm – a Welsh word meaning an enclosed valley on the side of a hill (pronounced coom)

Questions on the poem

1 Why is it so dangerous to climb Mount Everest?
2 In line 11 one of the climbers mentions a flag. Can you explain why they used flags? Think of the colour of the scene around them.
3 Look at the words that are repeated in lines 10, 13, 15 and 17. What do they tell us about Hillary and the other climbers?

PRE-READING ACTIVITY

In the poem 'The icefall', we read about brave climbers who overcame danger to reach the top of the mountain. Little John the Fearless faces very different dangers. You may also know of people who are brave in quite different ways. For example, is it easy to admit that you are wrong? Do you know anyone who is crippled or ill? Is this person always happy and friendly?

Little John the Fearless
Italo Calvino

There was once a little boy called Little John the Fearless because he was not afraid of anything. One day, as he was wandering through the world, he came to an inn and asked for a night's lodging.

"There is no room here," said the innkeeper, "but if you're not afraid I can send you to a deserted palace near by."

"And why should I be afraid?"

"Because there is a feeling about it, and no one has come out of there alive. Every morning a company of monks goes there with a coffin to carry away whoever had the courage to spend the night there."

You can imagine how Little John felt about this! He took along a lamp, a bottle of wine and a sausage, and went straight to the palace.

At midnight, while he was sitting at a table and having something to eat, he heard a voice from the top of the chimney: "Shall I throw it down?"

And Little John replied, "Go ahead, throw it down!"

A man's leg fell down the chimney. Little John drank a glass of wine.

Then the voice repeated, "Shall I throw it down?"

"Go ahead!" said Little John and another leg came down. Little John bit into the sausage.

"Shall I throw it down?"

"Go ahead!" And an arm came down. Little John started to whistle a tune.

"Shall I throw it down?"

"Go ahead!" Another arm.

"Shall I throw it down?"

"Go ahead!"

And the trunk of a man's body came down and attached itself to the arms and legs.

"Shall I throw it down?"

"Go ahead!"

A head came down and attached itself to the top of the body. It was a giant of a man, and Little John raised his glass and said, "Your health!"

The giant said, "Bring that lamp and come along with me."

Little John picked up the lamp but didn't move.

"Walk ahead of me," said giant.

"You go first," Little John replied.

"You!" said the giant.

"You!" said Little John.

So the giant went first. Passing from one room to another, they went right through the palace, while Little John walked behind with the light. Under the staircase there was a small door.

"Open it!" the man said to Little John.

And Little John said, "Open it yourself!"

So the man pushed it open with his shoulder. There was a spiral staircase.

"Go down," said the giant.

"You go down first," said Little John.

They went down into the basement. Pointing to a stone slab in the floor, the giant said, "Pick that up!"

"Lift it up yourself!" said Little John, and the man lifted it up as if it were a pebble.

Underneath the stone slab were three pots of gold. "Take them upstairs!" said the man.

"Take them up yourself!" said Little John. And the man carried them up one by one.

When they got back to the room with the chimney, the man said: "Little John, the spell is broken!" Then he took off one of his legs and it kicked its way up the chimney. "One pot of gold is for you," he said, as he took off one of his arms, and the arm climbed up the chimney. "The second pot is for the company of monks who will come to fetch you in the morning, thinking you are dead." He took off his other arm, and it followed the first one up the chimney. "The third pot of gold is for the first poor man who passes by," he said, as he took off his other leg and seated himself on the floor. "And this palace, you may keep for yourself," he said, as he removed the trunk of his body, leaving only his head on the floor, "because the owners have lost their claim to it for ever." Then his head disappeared up the chimney.

As soon as dawn came, a funeral chant was heard, "*Miserere mei, miserere mei.*" It was the company of monks with the coffin who had come to take away the dead Little John. But they saw him at the window, smoking his pipe.

With all that gold for himself, Little John the Fearless was a rich man and lived happily in the palace. Until one day it happened that, in turning round, he saw his own shadow and was so frightend by it that he died.

inn – hotel
deserted – empty, no one living there
monk – man living in a religious community
coffin – wooden chest in which a dead person is buried
trunk – body without the head, legs or arms
spiral staircase – stairs that wind around as they go upwards
pebble – small, smooth stone
chant – song

Questions on the story

1 What does the giant expect Little John to do when he appears from the chimney? What does Little John do? What would *you* have done?
2 When they walk through the palace Little John shows that he is clever as well as brave. How do we know this?
3 Did the author write this story to teach us
   (*a*) to appreciate courage?
   (*b*) to make us laugh?
   (*c*) to scare us?
   (*d*) all of these?
4 Many words in English have two or more different meanings. In this story "trunk" means a part of the body. What are the other meanings of this word?

12 Going home

Adventure

    It's not very far
        to the edge of town
    Where trees look up
        and hills look down.
    We go there
        almost every day
    To climb and swing
        and paddle and play.

    It's not very far
        to the edge of town
    Just up one little
        hill and down,
    And through one gate,
        and over two stiles —
    But coming home
        it's miles and miles.

Harry Behn

paddle – to walk in shallow water
stiles – steps made of wood allowing people to get over a fence

Questions on the poem

1 How do you spend your free time? Today, many children live in large cities. What games do they play after school?
2 What do the children in the poem do when they reach the edge of the town?
3 Which line tells us that there are steep hills nearby?
4 Read the last two lines of the poem again. Why is the journey home so long? What time of day is it?
5 Write two or three sentences on what you like to do during school holidays. You could start by telling whether you live in a city, a village or on a farm.

PRE-READING ACTIVITY

1 If you have younger sisters or brothers you probably have to take care of them when your parents are away from home. Have you ever had to protect them from unkind children? Have you ever been lost or felt that home is very far away?
2 Which of these sounds does a dog *not* make?
bark, whine, purr, whimper, growl.
3 Match the words in Column A with their meanings in Column B.

Column A   **Column B**
boulder   surprised
agonising   worried
terror   tiredness
amazed   rock
exhaustion   painful
anxious   fear

The new fire

Jenny Seed

Toma is a young Bushman whose parents and tribe have been killed. The attackers take Tu, Toma's little sister, with them on the long journey to the south. Toma follows them, determined to rescue Tu and return with her to their grandfather, Old Toma, their aunt Gokus and the only home they know.

He finds Tu sitting alone outside a hut. But before he can speak to her a dog barks, warning the attackers inside the hut that someone is nearby. Toma quickly hides in a small gap between two large rocks. Gun in hand, a man climbs the hill, his dog beside him.

Suddenly there was a crash so loud and so close that Toma jerked back in fright. Branches in the bush opposite the gap were shattered, scattering leaves and twigs and causing dust to rise up

73

into the air. There was another crash and another. Toma shut his eyes. But no harm touched him and dimly he understood that the man was firing into the bush in an attempt to drive out whatever might be hiding there and causing his beast to bark.

The noise of the weapon ceased. The man stood for a while as if waiting for some sound which might tell him what was lurking in the bush, then with an impatient click of the tongue, he walked away.

Looking quickly towards little Tu, he was amazed to see that she was still sitting just where she had been before the beast had begun to bark. And she was still staring blankly down at the sand. Toma understood then how it was with her. All the terror and the strangeness that had so suddenly come into her life had been too much for her. She was hiding within herself as surely as Toma was hiding within the bush.

And as he gazed at her, his mind slowly filled with despair and his courage failed. He felt so weak from the journey and the frightening ordeal he had just experienced, how could he hope to rescue little Tu?

With no courage to think about the future, he let his thoughts drift back into the past. He wanted to give up hope as he knew his sister had already given up hope.

Old Toma had known such weakness also. Toma seemed to hear again the words of his grandfather's song.

I am tired and old and my people have gone.
The wind has taken them away.
They were our people whom we loved.

Then as Grandfather's song echoed sadly in his head another picture formed in his mind. He saw the old man hunched over the little pile of grass and twigs beside the poor rough shelter which he had hastily erected after the disaster, twirling his firestick faster and faster in his thin hands until smoke began to rise and the first finger of orange flame had flared as it caught the dry grass. Toma could almost hear the snapping of the twigs and see the red tongues of flame licking at the wood as the new fire grew into a small blaze. That fire would still be alive.

The new fire, Toma thought. All was not dead. Across that great plain was a new fire with some of his own people waiting and watching for him. He lifted his head and looked again at Tu. The thought of his grandfather keeping the small fire burning in hope caused an answering hope to flicker suddenly in his own heart. Was there any way to rescue Tu? But how? He could not go to her without arousing the ferocious creature which guarded the dwelling. Tu would have to come to him. But how could he make her see him when she took no notice of anything but only stared down at the sand?

Deep in thought, Toma looked down and suddenly he saw his throwing stick which he had put with the arrows into his quiver when he and Grandfather had fetched what they needed from the old camp. He drew it out and felt the blackened pattern Tu herself had burnt down its length. Tu would know this stick. She would know that it was his and that he must be near. If he could throw it so that it landed in the sand close to her, it would make no noise and surely she would see it. But could he throw it such a distance? In the stick-throwing game boys had always used a mound to bounce their sticks forward.

Crawling back to the gap, he stared at the long grassy slope above the place where his sister was sitting. He saw that one of the huts in front hid her from the view of those in the dwelling. Looking again at the hill his heart gave a leap of excitement. There was a small anthill halfway down the slope.

Careful not to shake the branches of the bush in which he was hiding, Toma picked up his bow and quiver and the net of melons and stood up. Squeezing back through the narrow opening, he came out behind the boulders.

Putting down the net bag, he took the throwing stick from his quiver. Crouching, he gazed down at the mound. Holding the long stick firmly, he hurled it with all his might towards the grey anthill. He hardly dared to breathe as he watched it whirling silently through the air. It glanced off the hard mound, shooting forward, and landed not far from Tu in the soft sand.

Toma gasped with apprehension. It had not come as close to Tu as he had hoped, but he saw her lift her head suddenly as if the flight of the stick had caught her eye. She half turned her head, then to his dismay he saw that she had gone back to staring at the ground between her feet.

Little Tu! Toma wanted to shout her name. How could he wake

her from her dream of fear? As he knelt there, aware only of despair and disappointment, he saw her turn again, this time moving her body further round as if something about the flying stick and the soft sound it had made in landing was so familiar to her that she had gone on thinking of it. She stared at the long stick lying in the sand. Slowly and listlessly, she rose to her feet and walked towards it. Picking it up, she held it, turning it in her hand.

Toma was afraid that in her numbed state she might merely take the stick and walk away, but suddenly she looked up. It was a quick movement as if the meaning of the stick had at last reached her. She gazed in the direction from which it had come. Cautiously Toma waved his hand above his head.

Tu's mouth opened in astonishment when she saw him. Her eyes became large and alive in her little face. Instantly Toma pressed his finger to his lips to warn her to keep quiet, then beckoned to her to come to him.

With a lack of care that filled Toma with alarm, Tu began to run up the slope. Her small slender feet made no sound on the grass. As she climbed over the stone that hid him, Toma grasped her hand and, still stooping, ran with her down the hill on the other side.

"Run, little Tu!" he whispered, even now not daring to raise his voice, "Run!"

Keeping to the higher grassy ridges and the wide shelves of rock where their feet would leave no trail, they ran on until Tu could run no more. Still too fearful to stop so that she could rest, Toma picked her up and ran on, staggering under her weight and yet not daring to throw away the precious melons which could be the only moisture they might have until they reached the ostrich eggshell which he had buried.

At last even he could go no further. He sank down in the shade of a small tree and let Tu sit beside him. Panting, he glanced back, but there was no sign of anyone following them. He put his arm around his little sister, holding her closely, and stared ahead at the great waterless plain which they had to cross.

For a moment his courage threatened to leave him again, but he knew they could make the journey. They must make the journey. They had the melons and he had the digging stick and the hollow reed. They could find enough food and water. Besides, they had one another for company. Pressed against each other for warmth, they could live through another night of bitter cold.

And somewhere away in the distance to the north was the new fire which Old Toma had made.

"Tu," he said bravely. "We are going home. Grandfather and Gokus are waiting for us so that we may go together to find our kinsmen in the land where there is nothing but sun."

His little sister looked up at him with her large soft eyes. He saw by the great sadness in them that he had no need to tell her all that had happened, for she had seen more than he of the terrible attack. Instead she pressed even closer to him, her lips suddenly curving in a sweet trusting smile as she spoke for the first time since he had rescued her.

"Ai, Toma!" she said. "We are going home."

lurking – hiding and waiting
blankly – without interest
terror – fear
despair – without hope
ordeal – severe test
erected – built
disaster – suffering
ferocious – fierce
dwelling – place where people live
mound – small hill
with all his might – all his strength
glanced – slipped
apprehension – fear
dismay – feeling of fear
listlessly – too tired to show any interest
numbed – having no feeling
cautiously – carefully
astonishment – surprise
beckoned – called by moving the hand
staggering – walking unsteadily, nearly falling over
panting – taking very quick breaths
kinsmen – family

Questions on the story

1 What is the beast?
2 Why does little Tu just stare at the sand without moving?
3 When Toma nearly gives up his attempt to rescue Tu, what gives him courage to continue?
4 Why is Toma sure that Tu will recognize the throwing stick?
5 Explain why Toma is so pleased to see an anthill nearby.
6 The net bag Toma carries, contains melons. Can you explain why these are so important on his journey?
7 When they run away, why do they keep to the rocks?
8 What are Tu's first words to her brother?

13 Christmas

Kings came riding

Kings came riding
   One, two and three,
Over the desert
   And over the sea.

One in a ship
   With a silver mast;
The fishermen wondered
   As he went past.

One on a horse
   With a saddle of gold;
The children came running
   To behold.

One came walking
   Over the sand,
With a casket of treasure
   Held in his hand.

All the people
   Said "Where go they?"
But the kings went forward
   All through the day.

Night came on
  As those kings went by;
They shone like the gleaming
  Stars in the sky.

Charles Williams

mast – a long pole to support the sails of a ship
saddle – a seat for the rider of a horse
behold – watch
casket – a small box containing things of value

Questions on the poem

1 Soon it will be Christmas. In church, at school and on the radio Christmas carols will be sung. Do you know where you can read the story depicted in this poem and in 'Long, long ago'?
2 How does one know that the first king came from far away?
3 In verse 5 the people said, "Where go they?" How would we ask this question? Say where the kings are going.
4 The kings brought rich gifts to the Baby Jesus. If you could give a special gift to someone whom you love very much, what would it be?
5 Write five sentences about the things your family will do on Christmas Day.

Long, long ago

Winds through the olive trees
Softly did blow
Round little Bethlehem
Long, long ago.

Sheep on the hillside lay
Whiter than snow;
Shepherds were watching them,
Long, long ago.

Then from the happy sky
Angels bent low,
Singing their songs of joy,
Long, long ago.

For in a manger bed
Cradled, we know
Christ came to Bethlehem,
Long, long ago.

Anonymous

manger – a trough from which horses and cattle eat

Questions on the poem

1. Which words in verse 3 tell us that the birth of Jesus was a happy event?
2. The poet says that this happened long ago. Do you know how many years ago exactly Jesus Christ was born? Remember that our calendar is dated from the year of His birth.

3 Draw or paint a picture of the nativity scene. You could do this in small groups of eight or ten pupils. Two pupils could paint the background. Other pupils draw Mary, Joseph and the Baby Jesus, the Wise men and the shepherds. Remember the animals in the stable.

PRE-READING ACTIVITY

1 How do your mother and your teacher show that they are pleased with you, or cross with you? Think of the ways in which we use our bodies, our hands and faces to show how we feel.
2 Rewrite the sentences replacing the word in brackets.
Example
This bag is (heavy) than yours.
This bag is heavier than yours.
(a) This homework is the (easy) our teacher has ever given us.
(b) The new municipal offices are (ugly) than those across the street.
(c) Elizabeth is the (pretty) girl in the class.

The goldsmith's daughter
Ian Ferguson

Characters

THE GOLDSMITH
ELIZABETH
THE OLD WOMAN
ROBERT
TOWNSPEOPLE

Once upon a time, a long, long time ago, there lived a goldsmith who had one daughter. A good girl, but hideous to look at.
She was so hideous that she stayed at home and refused to go out, for if she did, people stared and laughed.

Her father gave her everything that she could desire, but Elizabeth, for that was her name, longed to be like other girls.
One day the housekeeper fell ill and Elizabeth had to go to town to buy food.

GOLDSMITH: Now Lizzie, be sure to bring home a fresh silver fish and crisp lettuce for our supper.
ELIZABETH: Yes, father.
GOLDSMITH: You are a good, kind girl Lizzie. People will see that in your face.
But Elizabeth did not believe him and, with her bonnet pulled over her face, she set out.
WOMAN: Who's that?
MAN: The Goldsmith's daughter.
WOMAN: Hideous!
MAN: Hilda!
Elizabeth wished she was safe back at home, but because she was an obedient girl, she hurried on to the market place and pretended she hadn't heard the cruel remarks. She bought a fish and some fresh green lettuce and then set out for home as fast as she could. The road home lay through a wood, and as she hurried along, weeping for her ugliness, she heard a voice calling her.
WITCH: Elizabeth! Elizabeth! Stop crying and come and help me.
ELIZABETH: Good day, old mother, what can I do for you?
WITCH: Alas, my dear, I have collected all these apples and now I find I cannot carry them. Will you help me? We poor people must struggle with little help or consideration, but rich men have both pomp and power and few rewards at the last hour.
ELIZABETH: I don't think I understand you very well, but let me help you for I have a straight back and young legs.
WITCH: Thank you, my child, my cottage isn't far at all.
With those words the old woman loaded the bag of apples onto Elizabeth's back.
WITCH: Light as a feather, how easily you manage!
ELIZABETH: No, indeed it isn't easy, but I *will* manage.
The bag grew heavier and heavier with each step that Elizabeth took.

ELIZABETH: These apples really are heavy. I can hardly breathe, let alone walk.

WITCH: Can you believe it, a strong girl like you complaining about a little bag that I have dragged around for years and years without complaining! Get a move on, I must get home. Lazy thing!

ELIZABETH: I must rest, just for a moment.

WITCH: What nonsense! When we reach my house, then you may rest, but not before.

Elizabeth felt her face grow red and she became very angry. She tried to lift the bag off her back, but it seemed to be stuck to her.

WITCH: Don't get angry, young lady! You offered to help me and now you must finish the job.

And with those words she jumped onto Elizabeth's back!

WITCH: Since you find it so comfortable, you can carry me too. Giddy up, you lazy thing!

At last they reached the old woman's cottage. She leapt off Elizabeth's back and then lifted the bag as easily as if it had been filled with feathers.

WITCH: Thank you, my dear, you have a kind heart. You shall be richly rewarded.

The old witch, for she was one, dug in her basket and produced a sunshade.

WITCH: Isn't that pretty, my dear? Would you like it for your very own?

ELIZABETH: Oh yes, but I don't have much use for the sunshade as I seldom leave my house.

WITCH: Just a minute, my dear. Hold the sunshade over your head.

A mirror gleamed in the old witch's hand, and in it Elizabeth saw the face of a beautiful woman.

WITCH: There you are! As long as you hold the sunshade over your head, nothing but the beauty of your heart will be reflected.

ELIZABETH: Oh! If only it could be mine!

WITCH: It is yours. I have given it to you. Now go and be happy.

ELIZABETH: May I give you something too? I see that life is hard for you, old mother, and this must be one of your most treasured possessions.

And she took off her gold bracelet that she loved dearly.

WITCH: Thank you, my dear. Goodbye.

And with that, the old woman closed her door and both she and her house vanished.

Elizabeth retraced her steps toward the town and, holding the sunshade over her head, she walked slowly down the street. Everyone who saw her was struck silent at the sight of her radiant beauty. She walked to the park where the young people were gathered together for a dance. She joined them twirling the sunshade over her. Everyone wanted to dance with her.

Suddenly the dancing stopped and she heard cruel laughter. The crowd had found a hunchback watching in the shadows.

1st: Be off with you!

2nd: Don't look Freddy, ugliness is catching.

elizabeth: Leave him alone, he hasn't harmed you!

Without thinking, Elizabeth handed the hunchback her sunshade. All at once he stood tall and proud.

all: Aahh!!

boy: What is your name, kind and lovely lady?

elizabeth: Elizabeth, sir.

boy: Beth.

1st: Give it to me!

2nd: No, I want to hold it first!

The strongest of the men caught the sunshade up and held it over his head and at once the cruelty of his heart showed on his face. He dropped the sunshade and fled to hide his ugliness from the light.

But Elizabeth and Robert, for that was the young man's name, had no further need for the sunshade which we give to you to use if you dare let people see what is in your heart.

---

hideous – very ugly
sunshade – object like an umbrella to protect one from the sun's rays
seldom – not very often
vanished – disappeared

Questions on the play

1 What does Elizabeth want more than anything else?
2 Elizabeth's father is a goldsmith and we read that she gives the witch a gold bracelet. What other gifts might her father have given her?
3 The goldsmith sends Elizabeth shopping. What does he think people will see when they look at her?
4 The witch tests Elizabeth. What does she do?
5 Why does Elizabeth feel sorry for the hunchback?
6 What is the storyteller trying to teach the reader?

Glossary

A
abyss – a very deep hollow
aisles – passages between the rows of pews in a chapel or church
alarm – fear, fright
amazed – surprised
amazing – surprising
amber spice – ripe, yellow fruit
annoyed – angry
apprehension – fear
approached – came near to
approve – agree with
apt – suitable
ark – the ship built by Noah that saved him from the Flood
astonishment – surprise
attach – join
authoritative – having the power to make others obey
avalanche – a mass of snow, ice and earth that falls swiftly down a mountain

B
banked – turned with one wing higher than the other
beckoned – called by moving the hand
behold – watch
belly – stomach
blankly – without interest
bliss – enjoyment, happiness
blunders – mistakes
boulders – large rocks
bow – rainbow
brace – support
brow – top

brute – cruel beast
budge – move
buttercups – small plants with yellow flowers

C

caddy – a small box containing tea
caraway bun – a bun with the seeds of the caraway plant
casket – a small box containing things of value
cautioned – warned
cautiously – carefully
cease – stop
chant – song
chanted – sang
chapel – a small church
chasm – deep opening in ice or rock
chores – household jobs
clogs – shoes carved from wood
coffin – wooden chest in which a dead person is buried
comfy – comfortable
courage – bravery
courted – loved
cowardly custard – frightened, lacking courage
cranny – a small hole or crack
crest – top
crevasse – deep opening in ice or rock
cringing – moving away in fear
crone – old woman
cwm – a Welsh word meaning an enclosed valley on the side of a hill (pronounced coom)

D

daisies – white flowers with yellow centres
damp – wet
deserted – empty, no one living there
desire – wish
despair – without hope
devoted – very interested in something
devotion – deep love
dire – dreadful, horrible
disaster – suffering

dismay – feeling of fear
doze – sleep
dubiously – in doubt
dwelling – place where people live

E
Earl Grey – a type of tea
earnest – serious
ecstatically – joyfully
eerie – strange and frightening
embarrassed – feeling uncomfortable
erected – built
extended – stretched out
extracted – took out

F
familiar – well known
fangs – long, sharp teeth
fell out – became bad friends
fender – piece of metal around a fireplace to prevent burning coal
          from falling onto the floor
ferocious – fierce
flannel – soft woollen cloth
flatter – praise very much
foes – enemies

G
gipsy – member of a race that has no permanent home
glanced – slipped
glittering – shining brightly
gobbled – ate very quickly and greedily
grindstone – stone shaped like a wheel, used to sharpen tools

H
half a crown – twenty five cents
hamper – large basket with a lid, used to contain food
harm – hurt
hauled – pulled
haunches – part of the body around the hips
heave – lift

hickory – a tree with very heavy wood
hideous – very ugly
hive – beehive, home for bees
hoisting – lifting
hole-y – having a hole in it
homestead – house or hut with the land around it
hushed – silent

I
I bet – I am sure
indignant – angry
inn – hotel
insolence – rudeness
intently – seriously
iris – plant with blue flowers
irritably – crossly

K
kinsmen – family
knead – to make flour and water into dough

L
larkspur – tall plant with white, pink or blue flowers
let out some more – allow more string into the air
listlessly – too tired to show any interest
lumber – to move clumsily and noisily
lurking – hiding and waiting
lustre-glossed – shining with a bright colour

M
maliciously – unkindly
manger – a box from which horses and cattle eat
mast – a long pole to support the sails of a ship
merrily – joyfully, happily
misery – unhappiness
monk – man living in a religious community
mound – small hill

N
nincompoop – foolish person
nook – a small, almost-hidden corner
numbed – having no feeling

O

of his own accord – without being asked or helped
ominous – threatening
ordeal – severe test
outwit – to get the better of someone by being cunning or clever
overtops – to rise above something

P

paddle – to walk in shallow water
panic – fear
panting – taking very quick breaths
party line – a telephone line that is shared by several people
peak – top of a mountain
peasant – someone who works on the land
pebble – small, smooth stone
peered – looked very carefully
perched – rested
pinnacle – peak, high part of a mountain
pitchfork – a long-handled fork used to lift hay
platter – large, flat dish
pleading – asking or begging for something
procession – a number of people following each other
prodded – pushed or poked
promptly – at once
prong – long pointed stick
puddles – small pools of rainwater
pullet – a young fowl
puncture – prick a hole in something

R

rage – anger
rain fell in torrents – heavy rain fell
rascal – mischievous person
ravine – deep valley
rear – back part
rickety – about to break
robin – a small red-breasted bird

S

saddle – a seat for the rider of a horse
sagging – sinking, hanging downwards
saliva – the liquid in the mouth

scornful – showing no respect
scruff of the neck – back of the neck
seldom – not very often
serac – hill of ice
serpent – snake
shedding feathers – letting feathers fall
shoving – pushing
show a leg – get out of bed
slight – unimportant
smarting – feeling painful
soared – flew high up in the air
sobbed – cried
soot – very small black pieces found in the smoke of fires
spiral staircase – stairs that wind around as they go upwards
splice – join
squirmed – twisted the body
staggering – walking unsteadily, nearly falling over
starving – dying of hunger
statue – stone figure of a person or animal
stiles – steps made of wood allowing people to get over a fence
stirring – moving
stock – animals
strike – hit
sunshade – object like an umbrella to protect one from the sun's rays
swirled – twisted
swooping – rushing
swot – crush, squash, destroy

T

terror – fear
thickets – trees and bushes growing very close together
thumped – beat, hit
timber – wood
tones – sounds of a voice
topsy-turvy – upside down
trough – a box from which animals drink or feed
trumpet – noise made by an elephant
trunk – body without the head, legs or arms
tyrant – cruel ruler

V
vanished – disappeared
veins – tubes that carry blood to the heart
vice – wickedness, naughtiness

W
"who're ye shov'n?" – Who are you pushing?
wig – false hair sometimes worn when a person is bald
wind dropped – the wind blew gently
with all his might – all his strength
wriggling – moving along by twisting to the left and right

Index of poets and authors

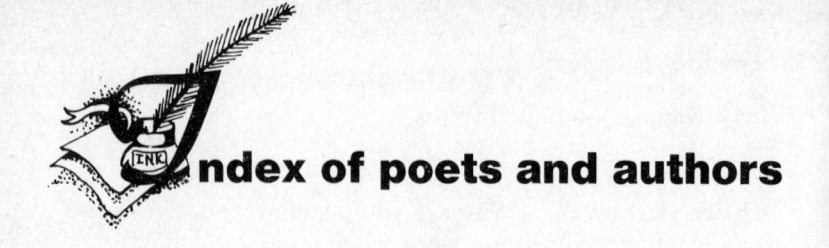

Ainsworth, Ruth 60
American Folk Rhyme 56
Anonymous 81
Behn, Harry 71
Belloc, Hilaire 30
Biegel, Paul 19
Calvino, Italo 67
Collodi, Carlo 38
Cresswell, Helen 31
Dahl, Roald 8
Dixon, Peter 36
Elliot, Geraldine 51
Farjeon, Eleanor 1, 50
Ferguson, Ian 13, 82
Field, Rachel 17
Macleod, Doug 29
O'Brien, Robert C. 45
Pitcher, Diana 2
Poland, Marguerite 24
Rands, William Brighty 11
Reeves, James 43
Rieu, E. V. 22
Rossetti, Christina 58
Seed, Jenny 73
Seraillier, Ian 6, 65
Williams, Charles 79

Acknowledgements

The compiler and publisher wish to thank all those who gave permission to reprint the material in this anthology. Acknowledgements are due to:

ELEANOR FARJEON 'The quarrel' and 'Nothing' from *Invitation to a mouse and other poems,* Knight Books.

DIANA PITCHER 'Dog' from *The calabash child,* David Philip, 1980.

IAN SERRAILLIER 'The icefall' and 'The kettle rhyme' from *Everest climbed* and *The monster horse,* Oxford University Press.

ROALD DAHL An extract from *Danny the champion of the world,* Jonathan Cape Ltd and Penguin Books Ltd, 1975. Permission granted by Murray Pollinger Literary Agent, London.

WILLIAM B RANDS 'Topsy-turvy world'

IAN FERGUSON 'The donkey, the miller and his son' and 'The goldsmith's daughter' from the entertainment *Confetti.* Permission from the author and the Dramatic, Artistic and Literary Rights Organisation (Pty) Ltd.

RACHEL FIELD 'Something told the wild geese' from *I will build you a house,* Hodder and Stoughton, 1984.

PAUL BIEGEL 'The timid starling' from *The elephant party and other stories,* Penguin Books, 1977.

E V RIEU 'Two people' from *A puffin quartet of poets,* 1958. Permission granted by executor of E V Rieu, Richard Rieu.

MARGUERITE POLAND 'Nombulelo' from *The Woodash stars,* David Philip, 1983.

DOUG MACLEOD 'Lovely mosquito' from *In the garden of bad things,* Penguin Books, Australia Ltd.

HILAIRE BELLOC 'The scorpion' from *The complete verses of H Belloc.* Permission granted by Pimlico, a division of Random Century.

HELEN CRESSWELL 'The gingerbread boy' from *At the stroke of midnight.* Traditional fairy tales retold by H. Cresswell, 1971.

PETER DIXON 'I'd like to be a teabag' from *Grow your own poems*, Macmillan Publishers. Permission granted by the author.
CARLO COLLODI An extract from *The adventures of Pinocchio*. Translated by Francis Wainwright, Octopus publishing group library. Methuen children's books.
JAMES REEVES 'Mrs Button' from *The wandering moon and other poems*, Puffin Books. Reprinted by permission of The James Reeves Estate.
ROBERT C O'BRIEN An extract from *Mrs Frisby and the rats of Nimh*. Acknowledgement Robert C O'Brien and Victor Gollancz Ltd.
GERALDINE ELLIOT 'The quarrel' from *The long grass whispers*, 1968. Reprinted by permission of the author and the Watkins-/Loomis Agency.
AMERICAN FOLK RHYME 'Old Noah's ark'.
CHRISTINA ROSSETTI 'Boats sail on the rivers'.
RUTH AINSWORTH 'The flood' from *The ten tales of Shellover*, André Deutsch Ltd, London.
ITALO CALVINO 'Little John the Fearless' from *Italian folk tales*. Translated by Sylvia Mulcahy. J M Dent and Sons Ltd Publishers.
HARRY BEHN 'Adventure' from *The little hill: Poems and pictures*. Copyright 1949 by H Behn, renewed 1977 by Alice L Behn. Reprinted by permission of Marian Reiner for the author.
JENNY SEED An extract from *The new fire*, Human and Rousseau, 1983. Permission granted by the author.
CHARLES WILLIAMS 'Kings came riding' from *I will build you a house*, David Higham Ass Ltd.
ANONYMOUS 'Long, long ago'.

Every effort has been made to trace the present copyright holders. If any copyright material is included for which permission has not been given, the compilers and the publishers wish to tender their apologies in advance to those concerned.